Charmaine S
Indian Cookbook
CHARMAINE SOLOMON

with lots of Love &
good wishes
from
Aunty Suha & Leeli
Mamu
15th sptub 1994

SPHERE BOOKS LIMITED
London and Sydney

First published in Great Britain by
Souvenir Press Ltd. 1981
Copyright © 1978 by Paul Hamlyn Pty Limited
Published by Sphere Books Ltd, 1984
30–32 Gray's Inn Road, London WC1X 8JL

TRADE
MARK

Set in Zapf

Printed and bound in Great Britain by
Cox & Wyman Ltd, Reading

Acknowledgements

I would like to thank those who made this book possible by helping in so many ways. My publishers and I are indebted to the hospitable people of India who gave their generous help and enthusiastic cooperation in the researching and gathering of material.

Though it is not possible to mention them all by name, when I look at this book I remember people from many different walks of life – from members of noble families to simple peasant folk. All had something to contribute. Rich and poor alike received me warmly, offered hospitality and showed me how to cook the specialities of their region.

Special thanks are due to the following organisations and their staff:

The Government of India Tourist Offices in Sydney, Delhi, Bombay, Agra and Madras.

State Government Officials in Rajasthan, Jammu and Kashmir, Goa, Daman and Diu, and Karnataka.

Air India and Indian Airlines.

Management and Chefs at Hotel Broadway, Srinagar; Hotel Ashoka, Delhi; Hotel Qutab, Delhi; Hotel Oberoi, Delhi; Hotel Mughal, Agra; Lake Palace Hotel, Udaipur; Shikarbadi Hotel, Udaipur; Hotel Oberoi, Bombay; Taj Mahal Hotel, Bombay; Fariyas Hotel, Bombay; Fort Aguada Beach Resort, Goa; Hotel Paraag, Bangalore; Temple Bay Beach Resort, Mahabalipuram; Silver Sands Beach Village, Mahabalipuram; Hotel Sudarshan, Madras; Hotel Dasaprakash, Madras; Taj Coromandel, Madras.

Preface

The finer points of Indian cooking have remained, for the most part, one of the mysteries of the mysterious East. Outside India, for better or worse, Indian food has come to be equated with curry. But curry is not just one dish, nor is every Indian dish a curry.

Reading this book, you will discover a cuisine as varied as the country's terrain. From the rich Kashmiri dishes of the snow-capped Himalayas to the simple vegetarian cuisine of the palm-fringed southern coasts, India offers a huge variety of cooking styles.

Although I grew up with Indian food as part of the scene, we made a special trip to India to collect material for this book, meeting cooks from all over the country and exploring as many different kinds of cooking as possible. I have tried to recreate this trip by indicating which part of India the recipes in this book come from, though there is no doubt that certain dishes have become so popular that they appear in places far from where they were evolved. Some staple foods, such as chapati and dhal, belong to the whole of India and so have not been attributed to one particular region.

I hope you enjoy this exploration of one of the world's great cuisines, and wish you as much pleasure in Indian cooking as I have found over the years and continue to find each time I cook an Indian meal.

Charmaine Solomon

Contents

Introduction

In describing the food of India it is necessary to make statements that seem contradictory but are all quite true. Some of the food is exotic and some is very simple. Some styles of cooking are based on meat and are very rich, while others are pure vegetarian and quite spartan. While certain dishes are hot, others are extremely delicate. Nowhere are contrasts in the cuisine of a country as striking as in India.

There are the Moghul-influenced dishes of the northern and central States. Most of these dishes are based on meat and cooked in clarified butter called ghee, and they use spices that are fragrant rather than pungent.

Intriguing hints of perfume (rose and another very fragrant essence called kewra) find their way into the Moghul dishes of Kashmir. While these are used to flavour sweets, it is surprising to find them in both meat and rice dishes. They are strangely pleasing and, of course, very subtle.

If you enjoy spicy, satisfying food that is not hot, choose from among the dishes of the north. Kashmiri chillies give rich, red colour but comparatively little heat, and paprika may be substituted. Some dishes do not use chillies at all and these are ideal for introducing children to the delights of Indian food.

North Indian curries, fragrant with saffron and rich with almonds or yoghurt are a far cry from the South Indian coconut milk curries, or the piquant Goan vinegar curries, or the hot Madras style curries. But there is more to Indian food than curries, as a glance through the recipes in this book will show.

I have also included some recipes from the Parsi cuisine, a very special style of cooking which has evolved since these people from Persia settled in India thirteen centuries ago.

The vegetarian food of India is undoubtedly the best in the world. Grains, lentils, milk products and seeds are combined to provide optimum nutrition. It is in South India that a pure vegetarian cuisine is outstanding.

Fish comes into its own along the coastal areas. It is the dishes of Bengal, Goa, Kerala and Maharashtra that include fish and shellfish cooked in many different styles, some delicate and others very hot. I remember a superb Prawn Masala served in Goa which used 50 dried chillies to spice 16 large prawns! When I tested the recipe I found 8–10 chillies quite sufficient, but if you are crazy about really hot dishes, adjust the amount of chilli to taste. But remember, hot and spicy dishes are meant to be eaten with a large amount of rice or bread if there are to be no regrets afterwards.

Rice and chapatis (unleavened wholemeal bread) are the staple foods, rice in the south and east, chapatis in the north and central areas. In the south, rice is mostly served plain boiled and it is served at every meal while in the north, when rice is used, it is for festive dishes like pilau and biriani.

Indian breads are a delight. There is a large variety and none of them are soft and bland. Most are whole wheat breads, firm and chewy in texture. Even those made with refined flour have far more character than the pallid white sliced loaf that the western world has come to accept as bread.

Since ovens are not part of the average Indian kitchen, most breads are cooked on a griddle by dry heat. Some are shallow fried, others are deep fried, but most highly regarded are those baked in the tandoor, a wood-fired earthen oven which imparts special flavour and provides the fierce heat necessary for leavened breads such as naan.

Accompaniments are an essential part of every Indian meal and there will always be two at the very least. They are easy to make and provide intriguing contrasts in flavour and texture which are most enjoyable.

India boasts a number of unique and delicious snacks made from the simplest ingredients. They are bought from the bazaars or from street sellers who specialise in one variety or another, or they may be made at home. They are mainly served at afternoon tea time, or between meals, but make ideal hors d'oeuvres or cocktail savouries.

While Indian meals do not necessarily include desserts, sweets of some sort are always served on festive occasions. Many Indian sweetmeats are made with vegetables or fruit as a base, for instance carrot, pumpkin or banana halwa. They are cooked with ghee, sugar and cardamom until of a firm, fudge-like consistency and often it is difficult to guess that the main ingredient is a vegetable.

In Agra, there is an industry that makes just one type of sweetmeat based on a special type of white pumpkin. Rows of shops deal in this single, very popular item called Petha. The process is quite complicated and necessitates a number of different procedures, but the end result is a delight. A crunchy cube or wedge of pumpkin with the flavour of rose has a juicy, translucent centre encased in a thin, crisp outer coat of crystallised sugar. The nearest equivalent in wester confectionery is glacé fruit and even that is a poor comparison.

Other sweets are made with lentil flour, almonds, pistachios, cashews, concentrated milk or fresh cheese. They may be firm and crisp, to be picked up in the fingers, or they may be soft and creamy and served in little dishes. Some are dry, some are syrupy, all are unusual but so delicious it seldom needs more than one taste to convince anyone that these are worth the calories.

The Magic and Mystique of Spicing

The art of spicing is valued above any other virtue in an Indian cook.

It may be surprising to the 'plain food' brigade that Indian food is very healthy. The spices and herbs used are credited with preventative and curative properties and the latest findings in medicine confirm that garlic and onions, almost universally used in Indian food, are useful in lowering cholesterol in the blood and controlling blood pressure. They are also rich in vitamins and trace elements.

Cinnamon and cloves are known to be germicidal. Coriander, cummin, nutmeg, mace, fennel and cardamom have carminative properties and are used to aid digestion. Chillies are very rich in Vitamin C and there are varieties, such as Kashmiri chillies, which are not pungent. Even hot chillies have a useful purpose. They are used mainly in parts of India where the temperature stays very high for most of the year. They stimulate the appetite, which tends to wilt in hot climates, but more importantly, they cause perspiration which cools the body by evaporation and also rids it of waste through the skin.

I was told by a Hindu gentleman very knowledgeable in these matters that the spicing of Indian food does not stem simply from the creativity of cooks. Rather, it is based on teachings laid down hundreds of years ago by medicine men and sages who believed that man is what he eats and therefore it was of supreme importance that food should be beneficial to physical and spiritual well being.

What is most noteworthy about Indian food is that every dish is spiced, yet no two dishes taste exactly alike. Contributing to this diversity is the fact that in India, commercial curry powders are not used. They are looked on with disdain and no cook worth his or her salt would be caught using them.

While commercial curry powder is made up of a number of different spices, it is made to a formula that remains inflexible.

On the other hand, working with individual spices, herbs and aromatic seeds, it is possible to produce a wonderful variety of dishes, each with its own distinct character, never boring to the cook or to the people who sit down to enjoy an 'original'.

It is this blending of spices that is the magic of Indian cooking. Even the humble potato can take on myriad different forms, depending on how simple or complex the *masala* used.

GUIDE TO INDIAN SPICES AND INGREDIENTS

The following ingredients will put the whole range of Indian spice dishes at your fingertips. Fresh ingredients are not included, only those that have a good shelf life. Buy in small quantities and store in airtight jars away from heat and direct sunlight.

AGAR-AGAR
Hindi: *chinai ghas*
A setting agent obtained from seaweed. Widely used in Asia, for it sets without refrigeration. Available in powder form from chemists or in packets from Asian grocers or health food stores. It is also sold in strands. Gelatine can be substituted, but texture will be different and the amount used varies.

AJOWAN
Bot.: *Carum ajowan*
Fam.: *Umbelliferae*
Hindi: *ajwain*
Of the same family as parsley and cummin, the seeds look like parsley or celery seeds, but have the flavour of thyme. It is used particularly in lentil dishes that provide the protein in vegetarian diets, both as a flavouring and as a carminative. It is one of the seeds used to flavour the crisp-fried snacks made from lentil flour. *Ajwain* water is used as a medicine for stomach ailments.

AMCHUR
Dried green mango, usually available in powder form. Used as an acid flavouring ingredient.

AROMATIC GINGER
Bot.: *Kaempferia pandurata* or *Alpinia officinarum*
Fam.: *Zingiberaceae*
Also known as 'galangal lesser', this member of the ginger family cannot be used as a substitute for ginger or vice versa. It is used only in certain dishes, and gives a pronounced aromatic flavour. When available fresh, it is sliced or pounded to a pulp; but outside of Asia it

is usually sold dried, and the hard round slices must be pounded with a mortar and pestle or pulverised in a blender before use. In some spice ranges it is sold in powdered form.

ASAFOETIDA
Bot.: *Ferula asafoetida*
Fam.: *Umbelliferae*
Hindi: *hing*
Tamil: *perunkaya*

Used in minute quantities, its main purpose is to prevent flatulence. It is obtained from the resinous gum of a plant growing in Afghanistan and Iran. The stalks are cut close to the root and the milky fluid that flows out is dried into the resin sold as *asafoetida*. Although it has quite an unpleasant smell by itself, a tiny piece the size of a pea attached to the inside of the lid of a cooking pot adds a certain flavour that is much prized, apart from its medicinal properties.

ATTA
Fine wholemeal flour used in making flat breads. Substitute fine wholemeal sold in health food stores. *Atta* flour can be bought from stores specialising in Asian foods.

BAGOONG
See Shrimp paste.

BAY LEAVES
Bot.: *Laurus nobilis*
Fam.: *Lauraceae*
Hindi: *tejpattar*

Used in North Indian cooking.

BESAN (CHICK PEA FLOUR)
Available at most shops selling Asian foods. Pea flour from health food shops can be substituted, but if it is coarse pass it through a fine sieve before using. Alternatively, roast yellow split peas in a heavy pan, stirring constantly and taking care not to burn them. Cool, then blend at high speed in an electric blender or pound with a mortar and pestle. Sift, then store the fine flour in an airtight container. *Besan* has a distinctive taste, and ordinary wheat flour cannot be substituted.

BOMBAY DUCK

Not a bird, despite its name, this is a variety of fish that is salted and dried. It is sold in packets and should be cut into pieces no more than 2.5 cm (1 inch) long. Deep fried or grilled, it is served as an accompaniment to a meal of rice and curry, and should be nibbled in little pieces.

CARDAMOM

Bot.: *Elettaria cardamomum*
Fam.: *Zingiberaceae*
Hindi: *illaichi*

Next to saffron, the world's most expensive spice. Cardamoms grow mainly in India and Sri Lanka and are the seed pods of a member of the ginger family. There are two varieties, the large, dark brown cardamom (*bara illaichi*) which is more pungent than the small, pale green variety (*chota illaichi*). This smaller variety is sometimes bleached in processing so that it looks almost white.

In India the brown cardamoms are preferred for certain curries and pickles, while in pilaus and sweets it is only the small green type which is used. Since the small variety is much more easily obtained, it is quite all right to use these in place of the larger ones in any recipe – they will impart a distinctive fragrance.

When ground cardamom is called for, the seed pods are opened and discarded and only the small black or brown seeds are ground. For full flavour, it is best to grind them just before using. There is one brand of 'ground decorticated cardamom' that seems to preserve extremely well the essential oils and fragrances of this exotic spice, but if you cannot buy a really good ground cardamom, crush the seeds in a mortar as required.

CASHEW NUT (CASHEWS)

Hindi: *kaju*

A sweet, kidney-shaped nut. In countries where the cashew tree is not grown, it is not possible to get the milky sweet fresh cashews. However, it is possible to buy raw cashews (as distinct from the roasted and salted cashews sold as snacks); nut shops, health food shops and groceries specialising in Asian ingredients stock the raw cashews.

CHAAR MAGAZ

Chaar means 'four' in Hindi and this is a mixture of four different seed kernels which are used like nuts in certain sweetmeats. The kernels come from the seeds of pumpkin, cucumber, watermelon and a type of marrow. Substitute raw sunflower seeds and untoasted pepitas.

CHILLI POWDER

Indian chilli powder is made from ground chillies. It is much hotter than the Mexican-style chilli powder, which is mostly ground cummin.

CHILLIES, PEPPERS

Bot.: *Capsicum frutescens* or *capsicum annum*
Fam.: *Solanaceae*
A much milder though still flavourful variety of chilli with a long pod large enough to stuff with spiced meat or fish mixtures.

CHILLIES, GOAN

A large, very dark red chilli which looks almost black when dried. It gives good colour to dishes in which it is used and is not as pungent as some of the smaller varieties of chilli.

CHILLIES, GREEN

Bot.: *Capsicum spp.*
Hindi: *sabz mirich*
Used like fresh red chillies. Sometimes ground into sambals. The seeds, which are the hottest parts, are usually (though not always) removed. See page xxxiv for advice on handling.

CHILLIES, KASHMIRI

Hindi: *degi mirich*
A red chilli of Kashmiri origin. They are less pungent than other red chillies.

CHILLIES, RED

Bot.: *Capsicum spp.*
Hindi: *lal mirich*
Tamil: *kochikai*
Used fresh for flavouring, either whole or finely chopped; or sliced for garnishes.

CHIRONJI or CHAROLI
A small, round nut with a brownish beige skin and a distinctive flavour. Used to give texture and flavour to sweets and certain savoury dishes. Substitute sunflower seeds or, more extravagantly, pistachio kernels.

CINNAMON
Bot.: *Cinnamomum zeylanicum*
Fam.: *Lauraceae*
Hindi: *darchini*
True cinnamon is native to Sri Lanka. Buy cinnamon sticks or quills rather than the ground spice, which loses its flavour when stored too long. It is used in both sweet and savoury dishes.
 Cassia, which is grown in India, Indonesia and Burma, is similar. It is much stronger in flavour, and is cheaper, but it lacks the delicacy of cinnamon. The leaves and buds of the cassia tree have a flavour similar to the bark and are also used for flavouring food.
 For sweet dishes especially it is best to use true cinnamon. Look for the thin pale bark, sun-dried to form quills that are packed one inside the other. Cassia bark is much thicker because the corky layer is left on.

CLOVES
Bot.: *Eugenia aromatica*
Fam.: *Myrtaceae*
Hindi: *laung*
Cloves are the dried flower buds of an evergreen tropical tree native to Southeast Asia. They were used in China more than 2,000 years ago, and were also used by the Romans. Oil of cloves contains phenol, a powerful antiseptic that discourages putrefaction, and the clove is hence one of the spices that helps preserve food. Use sparingly as cloves tend to overpower other flavours.

COCONUT MILK
Not the water inside the nut, as is commonly believed, but the creamy liquid extracted from the grated flesh of fresh coconuts or from desiccated (shredded) coconut. When coconut milk is called for, do try to use it, for the flavour cannot be duplicated by using any other kind of milk.

COCONUT VINEGAR

Made from the sap of the coconut palm which is matured in wooden barrels before being distilled. It is available where Asian ingredients are sold, but any light coloured mild vinegar may be substituted. If cider vinegar is used be sure to dilute with an equal amount of water.

CORIANDER

Bot.: *Coriandrum sativum*
Fam.: *Umbelliferae*
Hindi: *dhania* (seed), *dhania pattar, dhania sabz, hara dhania* (leaves)
Coriander seed, dried and ground, is one of the chief spices in Indian cookery. Fresh coriander is also used in Indian food, as widely as parsley is used in French and British cooking, not merely as a garnish but as an essential flavouring. Although it may be an acquired taste because of its pungent smell (the name coriander comes from the Greek *koris*, meaning 'bug'), it is indispensable in Indian dishes. To store the fresh herb which is sold in bunches complete with roots, do not wash or cut off the roots. Simply put into a plastic bag, eliminate as much air as possible and close the bag with a twist tie. It will keep, in the refrigerator, for more than a week. Wash just before using. When 'fresh coriander' is an ingredient in a recipe, use the leaves and the stalks, chopped.

If you have difficulty buying it, grow the herb yourself in a small patch of garden or even a window box. Scatter the seeds, sprinkle lightly with soil and water every day. The seeds take 18-21 days to germinate, but usually grow strongly when they do. Pick them when about 15 cm (6 inches) high and before the plants go to seed.

CUMMIN or CUMIN

Bot.: *Cuminum cyminum*
Fam.: *Umbelliferae*
Hindi: *sufaid zeera* (white cummin), *zeera, jeera*
Cummin is, with coriander, the most essential ingredient in prepared curry powders. It is available as seed, or ground. There is some confusion between cummin and caraway seeds because they are similar in appearance, but the flavours are completely different and one cannot replace the other in recipes.

CUMMIN, BLACK
Bot.: *Nigella sativa*
Fam.: *Ranunculaceae*
Hindi: *kala zeera, kàlonji*
Although the Indian name *kala zeera* translates as 'black cummin' this is not true cummin and the flavour is different. Aromatic and peppery, *Nigella* is an essential ingredient in *panch phora*.

CUMMIN, SWEET
See Fennel.

CURRY LEAVES
Bot.: *Murraya koenigii*
Fam.: *Rutaceae*
Hindi: *kitha neem, katnim, karipattar*
Tamil: *karuvepila*
Sold dried, they are as important to curries as bay leaves are to stews, but never try to substitute one for the other. The tree is native to Asia, the leaves are small and very shiny, and though they keep their flavour well when dried they are found in such abundance in Asia that they are generally used fresh. The leaves are fried in oil, until crisp, at the start of preparing a curry; they can also be pulverised in a blender; and the powdered leaves can be used in marinades and omelettes.

FENNEL
Bot.: *Foeniculum vulgare*
Fam.: *Rutaceae*
Hindi: *sonf*
Sometimes known as 'sweet cummin' as it looks like cummin but has a sweet liquorice flavour. It is available in ground or seed form. Substitute an equal amount of aniseed.

FENUGREEK
Bot.: *Trigonella foenum-graecum*
Fam.: *Leguminoseae* (papilionaceae)
Hindi: *methi*
These small, flat, squarish, brownish-beige seeds are essential in curries, but because they have a slightly bitter flavour they must be used in the stated quantities. They are especially good in fish

curries, where the whole seeds are gently fried at the start of cooking; they are also ground and added to curry powders.

GARAM MASALA
A mixture of ground spices used in Indian cooking.

GARLIC
Bot.: *Allium sativum*
Fam.: *Liliaceae*
Hindi: *lasan*
Almost universal in application, and vital in Indian cooking (although Kashmiri Brahmins eschew it as inflaming baser passions), garlic is not only a flavouring but is also prized for its health-giving properties.

GHEE (CLARIFIED BUTTER)
Sold in tins or plastic containers at many supermarkets and health food shops, *ghee* is pure butter-fat without any of the milk solids. It can be heated to much higher temperatures than butter without burning, and imparts a distinctive flavour when used as a cooking medium. If you find it difficult to buy *ghee*, make your own by heating unsalted butter until it melts and froths. Spoon off foam from the top and pour the melted butter into a heatproof glass bowl, discarding the milk solids in the pan. Leave to cool to room temperature, then chill until set. Spoon off the fat from the top, leaving residue. Heat the fat again, then strain through fine muslin to remove any remaining solids. This will keep for three or four months without refrigeration.

GINGER
Bot.: *Zingiber officinale*
Hindi: *adrak*
A rhizome with a pungent flavour, it is essential in many Indian dishes. Fresh ginger root should be used; powdered ginger cannot be substituted for fresh ginger, for the flavour is quite different. To prepare for use, scrape off the skin with a sharp knife, and either grate or chop finely (according to recipe requirements) before measuring. To preserve fresh ginger for up to three months, scrape the skin from the rhizome, divide into sections and pack in a well-washed and dried bottle. Pour dry sherry over to completely cover the ginger, cover tightly and store in the refrigerator.

JAGGERY
See Palm sugar.

KEWRA
See Pandanus odoratissimus.

KHOA
Unsweetened condensed milk made by boiling milk quickly in a shallow pan (such as a large, heavy frying pan) to allow for as much surface evaporation as possible. It must be stirred constantly. When ready, *khoa* has the consistency of uncooked pastry. Four cups of milk yield about 90 g (3 oz) of *khoa*. It is an ingredient in Indian sweetmeats and certain meat dishes.

A quick way to make *khoa:* measure 1 cup instant full cream milk powder into a bowl. Add 2 tablespoons water and mix to a stiff consistency. Yields 125 g (approximately 4 oz).

LIME, SMALL GREEN
Bot.: *Citrus microcapa*
Hindi: *nimboo*
The juice of this fruit is used in India mainly as a refreshing drink and also to add a sour flavour to certain dishes. Lemons may be used as a substitute.

MACE
Bot.: *Myristica fragrans*
Fam.: *Myristicaceae*
Hindi: *javatri*
Mace is part of the nutmeg, a fruit that looks like an apricot and grows on tall tropical trees. When ripe, the fruit splits to reveal the aril, lacy and bright scarlet, surrounding the shell of the seed; the dried aril is mace and the kernel is nutmeg. Mace has a flavour similar to nutmeg but more delicate, and it is sometimes used in meat or fish curries.

MINT
Bot.: *Mentha viridis*
Fam.: *Labiatae*
Hindi: *podina*
Although there are many varieties, the common, round-leafed mint is the one most often used in cooking. It adds flavour to many

curries, and mint chutney is a favourite accompaniment to a *biriani* meal or dipping sauce for *samosa*.

MUSTARD, BLACK
Bot.: *Brassica nigra*
Fam.: *Crucilerae*
Hindi: *rai, kimcea* (brown mustard)
This variety of mustard seed is small and more pungent than the yellow variety. Substitute brown mustard seed (*juncia*). Alba or white mustard is not used in Indian cooking.

MUSTARD OIL
Hindi: *sarson ka tel*
A pungent, deep yellow oil extracted from mustard seeds which is used predominantly in Bengal and in Kashmir. It is also used throughout India in certain recipes, particularly in making pickles as it is a preservative.

NUTMEG
Bot.: *Myristica fragrans*
Fam.: *Myristicaceae*
Hindi: *jaiphal*
Not widely used as a curry spice, but used to flavour some sweets and cakes, and sometimes used in *garam masala*. For maximum flavour, always grate finely just before using. Use sparingly, for large quantities (more than one whole nut) can be poisonous.

ONION
Bot.: *Allium cepa*
Fam.: *Liliaceae*
Hindi: *peeaz*
Onions come in many varieties. Those most commonly used in India are purple. Brown or white onions may be used instead.

PALM SUGAR
Hindi: *jaggery*
This strong-flavoured dark sugar is obtained from the sap of coconut palms and Palmyrah palms. The sap is boiled down until it crystallises, and the sugar is usually sold in round, flat cakes or two hemispheres put together to form a ball and wrapped in dried

leaves. Substitute black sugar, an unrefined, sticky sugar sold in health food shops, or use refined dark brown sugar sold at supermarkets.

PANCH PHORA
Panch means 'five' in Hindi, and *panch phora* is a combination of five different aromatic seeds. These are used whole, and when added to the cooking oil impart a flavour typical of Indian food.

PANIR
Home-made cream cheese. Bring milk to the boil, stirring occasionally to prevent a skin forming on top. As the milk starts to rise in the pan, stir in lemon juice in the proportion of 1 tablespoon to $2\frac{1}{2}$ cups milk. Remove from heat and let stand for 5 minutes, by which time firm curds will have formed. Strain through muslin. Let it hang for at least 30 minutes, then press to remove as much moisture as possible. If it has to be very firm, weight it down and leave for some hours in a cool place. This is necessary when it is cut into cubes and cooked with vegetable dishes, such as in *palak panir* on page 53. It may be added to any of the vegetable preparations for extra nutrition.

PANDANUS ODORATISSIMUS
Hindi: *kewra*
A variety of screwpine. The male inflorescence has a stronger perfume than roses or jasmine. It is used mostly in Indian sweets, and is obtainable as an essence or concentrate. It is so strong that only a drop is needed (or, more discreetly, a small skewer dipped in the essence is swished in the liquid to be flavoured). On special festive occasions, rose essence and kewra essence are used to flavour the rich rice dish, *biriani*.

Kewra water, a much milder flavouring, is also available at shops specialising in Indian ingredients.

PEPPER, BLACK
Bot.: *Piper nigrum*
Fam.: *Piperaceae*
Hindi: *kali mirich*
Pepper, the berry of a tropical vine, is green when immature, and red or yellow when ripe. Black pepper is obtained by sun-drying the

whole berry. It is only used in some curries, but is an important ingredient in *garam masala*.

PEPPERS, RED and GREEN
Bot.: *Capsicum grossum*
Hindi: *barra mirich*
Also known as 'capsicums' and 'sweet' or 'bell' peppers, this large, rounded variety is very mild and sweet in flavour, and is used as a vegetable or salad ingredient.

PISTACHIOS
Hindi: *pista*
The pistachio is a small, hard-shelled nut. When the pale brown shell is removed, the kernel is found to have a thin skin. This skin may be removed by blanching the nuts in boiling water for one minute, draining them, then slipping off the skin just as in blanching almonds. The nut itself is pale green and has a delicate and quite individual flavour. For the recipes in this book buy raw pistachio kernels not the toasted, salted pistachios that are sold in packets as snacks.

POPPY SEEDS
Bot.: *Papaver somniferum*
Fam.: *Papaveraceae*
Hindi: *khas-khas*
White poppy seeds are used in Indian curries mainly for thickening gravies since flour, cornflour or other starches are never used for thickening. The seeds are ground to a powder for this use. Black poppy seeds have a very different flavour so cannot be substituted. If unobtainable, use ground almonds as a substitute.

RED COLOURING POWDER
A brilliant red powder used very sparingly to give the distinctive colour seen in tandoori chicken and fish. Substitute paprika.

RICE FLOUR
Flour ground from raw rice. Used in making certain South Indian specialities.

RICE, GROUND

This can be bought at many grocery shops, health food shops and supermarkets, and is slightly more granular than rice flour. It gives a crisp texture when used in batters or other mixtures.

ROSE WATER

A favourite flavouring in Indian sweets, rose water is the diluted essence extracted from rose petals by steam distillation. It is essential in *gulab jamun* (page 154) and *ras gulas* (page 152), and is also used in *biriani*. If you use rose essence or concentrate, be careful not to over-flavour – count the drops. However, with rose water a tablespoon measure can be used. Buy rose water from chemists or from shops specialising in Asian ingredients.

ROTI FLOUR

Cream in colour and slightly granular in texture, this is ideal flour for all unleavened breads; unlike *atta* flour, it is not made from the whole grain. Sold at some health food and Asian grocery shops. It is also known as Continental flour or 'sharps', the grade to which it is milled.

SAFFRON

Bot.: *Crocus sativus*
Fam.: *Iridaceae*
Hindi: *kesar*

The world's most expensive spice, saffron is obtained by drying the stamens of the saffron crocus. The thread-like strands are dark orange in colour and have a strong perfume; it is also available in powder form. Do not confuse it with turmeric, which is sometimes sold as 'Indian saffron'. Beware also of cheap saffron, which in all probability will be safflower or 'bastard saffron' – it looks similar, and imparts colour, but has none of the authentic fragrance. Saffron is used more extensively in northern India than anywhere else in Asia. If using powdered saffron, use only half as much by volume.

SEMOLINA

Hindi: *soojee*

A wheat product which comes in coarse, medium and fine grades. Recipes stipulate the correct grade to use, but a different grade can be substituted although there will be some change in texture.

The bulk semolina sold in health food shops is medium grade; and the packaged semolina sold in Italian delicatessens is either medium or very fine. A little experimental shopping is recommended, for the grade of semolina is seldom on the label.

SESAME OIL
Hindi: *til-ka-tel*

Sesame oil used in Indian cooking is light. The more readily available sesame oil used in Chinese cooking is extracted from toasted sesame seeds, and gives a different flavour. If unable to buy light sesame oil use 1 teaspoon dark sesame oil to 1 tablespoon vegetable oil.

SHALLOTS
Bot.: *Allium ascalonicum*

Shallots are small, purplish onions with red-brown skin. Like garlic, they grow in a cluster and resemble garlic cloves in shape.

SHRIMP PASTE or BAGOONG
Tagalog: *bagoong*
Indonesian: *petis*

Although not widely distributed as *bagoong* or *petis*, this is sold as 'shrimp sauce' or 'shrimp paste'. Thick and greyish in colour, with a powerful odour. Substitute dried shrimp paste (blachan) or anchovy sauce.

SILVER LEAF
Hindi: *varak*

This edible decoration for festive pilaus and sweetmeats is made from real silver. Small pieces of silver are interleaved with sheets of tissue and a number of these wrapped in heavy leather and beaten repeatedly until of extreme fineness. Flutter on to the dish by holding the sheets of tissue. No substitute.

SPRING ONIONS
Bot.: *Allium cepa* or *Allium fistulum*
Fam.: *Liliaceae*

Spring onions are the thinnings of either *Allium cepa* or *A. fistulum* plantings that do not form a bulb. They are white and slender, with green leaves.

SPRING ROLL PASTRY
Thin white sheets of pastry sold in plastic packets and kept frozen.
Thaw and peel off one at a time (unused wrappers can be re-frozen).
Available at Chinese delicatessens.

TAMARIND
Bot.: *Tamarindus indica*
Fam.: *Leguminoseae*
Hindi: *imli*
This acid-tasting fruit of a large tropical tree is shaped like a large
broad bean and has a brittle brown shell, inside which are shiny
dark seeds covered with brown flesh. Tamarind is dried, and sold in
packets. For use as acid in a recipe, soak a piece the size of a walnut
in half a cup of hot water for 5–10 minutes until soft, then squeeze it
until it mixes with the water and strain out the seeds and fibres.
Tamarind liquid is used in given quantities. Tamarind is also
available in instant form which is more concentrated. Use a quarter
of the amount if substituting for tamarind pulp and dissolve in hot
water. Substitute lemon juice.

TANDOORI MIX
*A blend of hot and fragrant spices including cardamom, chillies,
turmeric, saffron, and garam masala.* If commercial brands are not
available, substitute the mixture given on page xxx. A half teaspoon
of garlic powder can be added, but this is not necessary if fresh
garlic is used in the recipe.

TULSI
Bot.: *Ocimum sanctum*
Hindi: *tulsi, tookmeria*
This is the tiny black seed of a plant of the basil family. The seeds
look like poppy seeds when dry, but when soaked in water they
develop a slippery, translucent coat. They are floated on cool, sweet
drinks, for they are said to cool the body (a highly regarded attribute
in hot countries); and although without flavour, they add an
intriguing texture.

TURMERIC
Bot.: *Curcuma Longa*
Fam.: *Zingiberaceae*
Hindi: *haldi*
A rhizome of the ginger family, turmeric with its orange-yellow colour is a mainstay of commercial curry powders. Though often called Indian saffron, it should never be confused with true saffron and the two may not be used interchangeably.

YOGHURT
In India this is called *dahi* or curd and is always unflavoured. Natural yoghurt should be used, and if possible choose one with a definite sour flavour. I have found that goat-milk yoghurt or Greek yoghurt is most suitable.

SPICE MIXTURES AND CURRY PASTES

Masala is a word that means a blend of spices. There are dry *masalas* in powder form and wet *masalas* in the form of a paste ground with water, vinegar or oil. But it is good to be able to choose for yourself exactly what will go into that spice blend.

There are some that may be made up and kept ready because they are used frequently. *Garam masala* is an example, but there are different kinds of *garam masala*. There is *garam masala* with pepper, *garam masala* with only fragrant spices and so on. Depending on the dish you are making and on your own taste or the preference of those you are cooking for, choose one or the other to give the finishing touch.

Because cloves, cardamom, cinnamon, the main ingredients of *garam masala*, take time and effort to grind, it makes sense to process enough to last for a while and store it in an airtight container away from heat and sunlight so it will not lose its fragrance.

Make up a few different spice blends and have them on hand, but don't use them in the same combination or proportions every time. Have individual spices on hand so that you can 'do your own thing', departing from a recipe as your creativity demands.

A few rules to remember will help, as will getting to know the aroma and flavour characteristics of each spice.

For instance, clove is used in very small quantities because it is strong and overpowers other flavours.

Cardamom, while it may be used more generously, is still to be handled with economy.

Saffron, the world's most expensive spice, lends a richness and perfume that cannot be imitated or approximated by substitutes, but it must be used with restraint. When a measurement is an eighth or a quarter of a teaspoon of saffron strands, just drop them loosely into the measure – don't pack them in. Pound in a mortar to crush them and dissolve in a small amount of boiling water before adding to a recipe. *If using powdered saffron, reduce the amount by half.* Kashmir and Spain produce the world's best saffron and it is expensive. Beware of imitations or saffron which has been adulterated (see Guide to Indian Ingredients, page xxv).

Spices that are used in greater quantity are coriander with its warm, comforting aroma and cummin with its mild, lemony tang. Sweet cummin or fennel seed is to be used in smaller quantities than either of these two, for it has a liquorice-like sweetness that can easily be overdone, though in the correct proportions it gives an enchanting fragrance.

Fenugreek, with its slightly bitter taste and strong smell, is used ground in many dishes, but again must be used discreetly.

Then there are the whole seeds used for flavouring – black mustard, black cummin, ajowan, fenugreek, fennel and cummin. There is a most useful combination of five different seeds, *panch phora*, which is used mainly for vegetable preparations. The proportions are important, some of these seeds being much more strongly flavoured than others. See page xxxi for *panch phora* recipe.

Curry is not necessarily hot. It is only when hot chillies or chilli powder are included in excessive amounts that a curry becomes hot. In small amounts, chilli adds inimitable flavour and stimulates the appetite without causing discomfort. A whole or split and seeded fresh chilli is one of the best ways of imparting flavour.

Herbs, dried or fresh, are those accents which the creative cook should never be without. *Tejpattar* (bay leaf) *kari pattar* (curry leaves) *methi* (fenugreek leaves) and coriander are available dried, while fresh coriander and mint may be bought at some greengrocers or easily grown in a patch of earth or a window box.

The following recipes are for some of the most commonly used *masalas.*

GARAM MASALA *(Ground Mixed Spices)*

There are many versions of garam masala, some using hot spices, such as pepper, and others only the fragrant spices. Here are some combinations to choose from according to your own personal taste. Made from good quality spices and stored airtight, garam masala will keep its flavour and fragrance for months.

No. 1 Garam Masala

4 tablespoons coriander seeds
2 tablespoons cummin seeds
1 tablespoon whole black
  peppercorns
2 teaspoons cardamom seeds
  (measure after roasting and
  removing pods)

4 x 7.5 cm (3 inch) cinnamon
  sticks
1 teaspoon whole cloves
1 whole nutmeg

In a small pan roast separately the coriander, cummin, peppercorns, cardamom pods, cinnamon and cloves. As each one starts to smell fragrant turn on to plate to cool. After roasting, peel the cardamoms, discard pods and use only the seeds. Put all into electric blender and blend to a fine powder. Finely grate nutmeg and mix in. Store in glass jar with airtight lid.

No. 2 Fragrant Spice Garam Masala

3 x 7.5 cm (3 inch) cinnamon
  sticks
2 teaspoons cardamom seeds
  (measure after removing pods)

1 teaspoon whole cloves
1 teaspoon blades of mace, or
  ½ nutmeg, grated

Roast spices separately and grind in a blender or with mortar and pestle; add grated nutmeg, if used.

No. 3 Kashmiri Garam Masala

2 teaspoons cardamom seeds
  (measure after removing pods)
1 teaspoon black cummin seeds
1 teaspoon whole black
  peppercorns

2 x 5 cm (2 inch) cinnamon
  sticks
½ teaspoon whole cloves
quarter of a nutmeg, grated

Roast spices separately and grind to a fine powder. Add nutmeg. Store in an airtight container.

MADRASI MASALA *(Madras Style Curry Paste)*

1 cup ground coriander
½ cup ground cummin
1 tablespoon each ground black
  pepper, turmeric, black
  mustard, chilli powder, and
  salt

2 tablespoons each crushed
  garlic and finely grated fresh
  ginger
vinegar for mixing
¾ cup oil

Combine ground spices and salt in a bowl. Add garlic and ginger and sufficient vinegar to mix to a smooth, thick purée. Heat oil in saucepan and when very hot turn in the spice mixture and reduce heat. Stir constantly until spices are cooked and oil separates from spices. Cool and bottle. Use about a tablespoon of this paste for each 500 g (1 lb) of meat, fish or poultry, substituting it for the garlic, ginger and spices in a recipe.

PANCH PHORA

'Panch' means five in Hindi and panch phora is a combination of five different aromatic seeds. These are used whole.

2 tablespoons black mustard
  seed
2 tablespoons cummin seed

2 tablespoons black cummin
  seed
1 tablespoon fenugreek seed
1 tablespoon fennel seed

Put into a glass jar with a tight fitting lid. Shake before use to ensure even distribution.

TANDOORI MIX

A blend of hot and fragrant spices. It may be purchased in bottles.

2 teaspoons turmeric
1 teaspoon paprika
½ teaspoon chilli powder
  (optional)
1 teaspoon garam masala
  (page xxx)

½ teaspoon ground cardamom
⅛ teaspoon powdered saffron,
  optional
½ teaspoon garlic powder

Thoroughly mix the ingredients.

TAAZA MASALA (*Green Masala Paste*)

A spice paste based on fresh coriander leaves, mint, garlic and ginger. Added to any curry or spiced preparation, it will give extra flavour. It may also be purchased in bottles.

1 teaspoon fenugreek seeds
3 teaspoons chopped garlic
2 tablespoons chopped fresh ginger
1 cup firmly packed fresh mint leaves
1 cup firmly packed fresh coriander leaves

½ cup vinegar
3 teaspoons salt
2 teaspoons ground turmeric
½ teaspoon ground cardamom
½ cup vegetable oil
¼ cup sesame oil

Put fenugreek seeds in water to soak overnight. They will swell and develop a jelly-like coating. Measure 1 teaspoon of soaked seeds and put into container of electric blender with garlic, ginger, mint, coriander and vinegar. Blend on high speed until very smooth. Mix in salt and ground spices. Heat oils until very hot, add blended mixture, bring to boil, turn off heat. Cool and bottle. Oil should cover the top of the herbs. If there is not quite enough oil, heat a little more and add it to the bottle.

Indian Cooking Made Easy

It is not difficult for Western cooks to make traditional Indian dishes in their own kitchens, and the results are usually highly satisfactory. Preparation need not take a long time, either. Here are some time-saving shortcuts in the preparation and measuring of ingredients.

GINGER, GARLIC AND ONIONS

When measuring garlic and ginger (and most Indian recipes use one or the other if not both) it is easier to get an accurate measurement in spoonfuls. Cookbooks used to have instructions to chop or grind a 2 cm or 5 cm (1 inch or 2 inch) piece of fresh ginger. A ginger root can be as slender as your little finger or twice as thick as your thumb, so it leaves too much room for variation. Garlic cloves can be as large as a chestnut, as slim as an almond or as small as a pistachio. To achieve uniformity I have measured garlic and ginger in spoonfuls, chopped. They do not need to be too finely chopped if they are to be ground in a blender after measuring. Chop only enough to be able to measure in a spoon.

I sometimes recommend finely *grated* ginger and this is a useful method if the ginger is mature and fibrous – all the fibres are left on the outside of the grater and can be discarded. Grating is particularly useful if you don't have an electric blender or if you need only a very small quantity. Choose the right grater surface – not the one for grating cheese or lemon rind and not the large shredder, but the small version of the shredder. This gives a very satisfactory result.

When I wrote my *South East Asian Cookbook* five years ago I advocated the use of an electric blender with a powerful motor and a glass container as being the best substitute for the grinding stones used in the East. I still feel it is the most essential piece of kitchen equipment for anyone who wants to cook Asian food in a Western kitchen.

It grinds spices, coconut and rice. It blends chillies, onions, garlic, ginger and other ingredients to a smooth purée.

Recently, with more recipes than usual being tested and re-tested in my kitchen, I had to cut down on preparation time. The peeling and chopping or crushing of garlic and ginger is one of those ever-recurring tasks. I have used the electric blender to grind a week's supply of ginger and of garlic (separately), using mild white vinegar to facilitate blending. These I store in screw-top jars in the refrigerator. In this form they are easy to measure in spoons. This may be a useful hint for others who use these ingredients frequently and find it time-consuming to prepare the small amounts each time.

There is one job, however, that the electric blender cannot do, and that is to chop onions without crushing them. The chopping of onions is a task ever-present in Indian cooking and many's the time I have stood, quite happy in my work, but with tears streaming from my eyes.

I have tried every suggestion passed on by fellow sufferers and to date the most effective method is to hold a small teaspoon or a match between the teeth. Why this helps I do not know – it just does, though I was incredulous too when first told about it. It also helps to use a knife that is not only sharp but which also has a very thin blade (like a Chinese chopper) so that the tissues of the onion are not crushed releasing fumes, but cleanly sliced through.

When roughly chopped onions are specified, cut them only enough to enable the blender to work on them.

When onions are to be sliced, it does not mean they have to be cut in perfect rings. All you need do is peel the onion, cut in halves lengthways and place the cut surface down on a wooden board before slicing it either crossways or lengthways – much easier than trying to slice an onion with a slippery, curved surface against the board. For the one or two recipes in this book that do require onion rings, cut a small slice from one side of the peeled onion and use this as a base when slicing.

To introduce some uniformity in judging the size of onions, here is a guide. A large onion is one that weighs over 250 g (8 oz); a medium onion is about 125 g (4 oz); a small onion weighs in around 60 g (2 oz). Weigh some onions to get an idea of the sizes and it will save you much deliberation.

CHILLIES
Fresh chillies: These are used in many Indian dishes. For mild flavouring simply wash the chilli and add it to the dish when simmering, then lift out and discard the chilli before serving. But if you want the authentic fiery quality of the dish and decide to use the chillies seeded and chopped as the Indians do, then equip yourself with disposable plastic or well-fitting rubber gloves.

Remove stalk of chilli and make a slit to remove the seeds,

scraping them out with the tip of a small, sharp knife; or, cut the chilli in two lengthways and remove the central membrane together with the seeds. The seeds are the hottest part of the chilli.

If you cut or chop chillies without gloves, wash your hands thoroughly with soap and warm water afterwards. Chillies can be so hot that even two or three good washings do not stop the tingling sensation, which can go on for hours. If this happens, remember to keep your hands well away from your eyes, lips or where the skin is especially sensitive – and in particular, don't touch young children.

Dried chillies: There are large and small dried chillies; those called for in the following recipes are the large variety. If frying them as an accompaniment to a meal, use them whole, dropping them straight into hot oil. If they are being soaked and ground, first break or snip off the stalk end and shake the chilli so that the seeds fall out. They are safe enough to handle until they have been soaked and ground, but if you handle them after this has been done, remember to wash your hands at once with soap and water. Dried chillies, though they give plenty of heat and flavour, do not have as much effect on the skin as fresh chillies with their volatile oils.

COCONUT MILK AND GRATED COCONUT

In India, fresh grated coconut is used to garnish some dishes. If coconuts are available, fine. If not, use desiccated coconut and sprinkle a little water on it, tossing until evenly moistened. Leave to stand for a few minutes and it will be a good substitute for freshly grated coconut. It should not be wet, just moist.

Coconut milk is not the clear liquid in the nut, though many people seem to think so. The clear liquid is good for drinking, but coconut milk is a different proposition – very rich in fats and therefore useful for enriching dishes of all kinds. It is extracted from the freshly grated white meat of the mature coconut and when this is subjected to pressure, the rich liquid which is coconut milk is obtained.

The first extract is known as 'thick coconut milk' and the second extract as 'thin coconut milk'. Unless one or the other is called for, use a mixture of first and second extracts.

When either thin or thick milk is specified, you will find they are usually added at different stages of a recipe, the thick milk being added at the end.

Using fresh coconut: If you have access to fresh coconuts and the use of a coconut grater you are well on the way to the best coconut milk. There are various types of coconut graters; the most successful one, and the easiest to use, screws on to the edge of a table, like a mincing machine. It has a number of curved, serrated blades that meet at a central point like a citrus juice extractor. By turning the handle with one hand and holding a half coconut in position with the other, it is possible to grate all the white flesh with no danger of slipping knives or skinned knuckles.

However, if you are able to get fresh coconuts and do not have this sort of implement, use the electric blender both to pulverise the coconut and to extract the milk. First crack the nut in two by hitting it several times with the back of a heavy kitchen chopper around the middle of the nut. Once a crack has appeared, insert the thin edge of the blade and prise it open. Save the sweet liquid inside for drinking. Put the two halves of the nut into a low oven and in 15 or 20 minutes the flesh will start to come away from the shell. Lift it out with the point of a knife, and peel away the thin dark brown skin that clings to the white portion. Cut into chunks, put into container of electric blender with 2 cups milk or water and blend at high speed until coconut is completely pulverised. Strain out liquid, repeat using more water and the same coconut.

To extract fresh coconut milk by hand, grate the pieces of white meat finely and to each cup of grated coconut add a cup of hot water, knead thoroughly and strain out the liquid. Repeat process a second and even a third time, adding hot water.

Using desiccated coconut: Many cooks use desiccated coconut for making milk. Nine times out of ten I do, too. It is much easier and quicker to prepare than grating fresh coconut, and in curries you cannot tell the difference.

Put 2 cups desiccated coconut in a large bowl and pour over $2\frac{1}{2}$ cups hot water. Allow to cool to lukewarm, then knead firmly with the hand for a few minutes and strain through a fine strainer or a piece of muslin, squeezing out as much liquid as possible. This should produce approximately $1\frac{1}{2}$ cups *thick* coconut milk.

Repeat the process using the same coconut and $2\frac{1}{2}$ cups more hot water. This extract will yield approximately 2 cups *thin* coconut milk. (Because of the moisture retained in the coconut the first time, the second extract usually yields more milk.)

Using a blender: With an electric blender you save time and a lot of hard work. Put 2 cups desiccated coconut and 2½ cups hot water in blender container, cover and blend for 30 seconds. Strain through a fine sieve or piece of muslin, squeezing out all the moisture. Repeat process, using the same coconut and 2½ cups more hot water.

Sometimes a richer milk is required. For this, hot milk replaces the water and only the first extract is used. However, a second extract will yield a flavourful and reasonably rich grade of coconut milk that can be used in soups, curries or other dishes.

Using creamed coconut: For an all-purpose coconut milk dissolve 30 g (1 oz) creamed coconut in ¾ cup hot water.

OIL AND GHEE

With today's emphasis on weight control I have made modifications in the quantity and type of fat used for cooking. I have found it is possible to get very good results using only half the amount of fat called for in many traditional dishes.

Ghee, which is clarified butter, is the main cooking medium in North India. It keeps without refrigeration because it is pure butter fat with all the milk solids removed. It is essential both for flavour and for its ability to reach high temperatures without burning. I use it for flavour, but substitute light oils for a proportion of the ghee.

Utensils for Indian Cooking

The brass *degchi* used throughout India is like a saucepan without handles. The sides are straight and have a horizontal rim. The flat lid fits over the rim of the pan, and is sometimes sealed with a flour and water paste, making a sort of oven or steam cooker out of the pan, for what is called *dum* cooking. Hot coals are put on the lid to provide cooking heat from above as well as below, for ovens are almost unknown in the average Indian household. Nowadays the *degchi* is also made from aluminium.

The Western housewife with her gas and electric appliances can cook any kind of food with less effort than can the Indian housewife with her primitive equipment.

Saucepans with well-fitting lids are just as suitable as a *degchi*, and a casserole in the oven is the answer to *dum* cooking. Wooden spoons substitute for the coconut-shell spoons mostly used in India, and a deep frying pan takes the place of the *karahi*, a rounded pan used for frying. A Chinese *wok* is the same shape as a *karahi* and makes a good substitute. Stainless steel woks are not recommended. The 30-35 cm (12-15 inch) *wok* is most useful.

A griddle or heavy iron plate replaces the *tawa* on which *chapati* or *paratha* are cooked; even a heavy frying pan will do. The ever-present grinding stone for spices, and the coconut grater, are replaced by the versatile electric blender; failing that, use a mortar and pestle for spices.

Serving an Indian Meal

For family dining and intimate entertaining the *thali* service is generally used. The *thali* is a circular tray of silver, brass or stainless steel set before each person on which are a number of small bowls called *katoris*. Rice, *chapatis* or other 'dry' foods are placed directly on the *thali* while the liquid dishes are served in *katoris*.

In South India, fresh banana leaves frequently replace the *thali*, especially in restaurants. And in a home in Karnataka we were served a meal on plates made of pretty circular leaves joined together. Little clay cups are used for the various curries, *dhals*, yoghurt and other accompaniments. These are thrown away after being used once.

Food is eaten with the fingers of the right hand only, the left hand being considered 'unclean', but styles of eating vary. North Indians are very particular about using only the tips of the fingers. They frown on the 'all in' approach that many southerners adopt, when it is considered all right to use the whole hand, even the palm.

It is always easier to eat Indian breads with the fingers. How else can you manage to tear off a piece of *chapati*, scoop up curry or roll a piece of kebab in it and convey it to your mouth? Knives and forks were just not intended for this kind of food.

When entertaining Western guests Indian hosts provide spoons and forks and dinner plates, though orthodox Hindus consider that crockery and cutlery that is used again and again is unhygienic.

Rice is served first in the centre of the plate and various curries and accompaniments are placed around it. It is wrong to mix the rice and all the accompanying dishes together though some people have the mistaken notion that this is how it should be done.

Imagine a carefully cooked meal, each dish with its own characteristics, and then someone comes along and jumbles the whole thing up! It shouldn't happen to any hostess. Correctly, and for greatest enjoyment, only one curry should be tasted with each mouthful of rice in order to appreciate the individual spicing of each dish.

Unlike Western meals where a large portion of meat or fish or poultry is eaten with a small amount of rice, Indian meals place emphasis on the rice. There are two reasons. Firstly, meat, fish or poultry is not the main dish, rice is. Secondly, the meat dishes will be spiced and rich and the only way to appreciate spiced food is with the bland background provided by the rice, *chapatis* or *naan*. It is also much easier on the digestion.

A non-vegetarian meal centres on rice or *chapatis* served with two or more dishes in which the main ingredient is meat, poultry or seafood. There will be various vegetable preparations, some dry, some with gravy and at least two (often more) accompaniments. A soup is sometimes served with the meal, not as a first course.

Vegetarian meals, too, are based on rice or *chapatis* and in some areas, particularly Gujarat, both rice and some kind of Indian bread, perhaps *puris*, are served together. Lentils or dried beans and green, yellow or leafy vegetables will be cooked, some with gravy and others in a dry style. Dishes of soupy consistency are presented in individual serving bowls called *katoris*. Fresh cheese, yoghurt or buttermilk will feature in a spicy preparation and in addition there is always a small bowl of plain yoghurt provided for each diner. Crisp fried *pappadams*, hot pickles and fresh chutneys are invariably offered.

There are strong feelings and much argument about what to drink with Indian meals, but these are only among foreigners. Indians mostly drink cold water and say little on the subject. There are Westerners who insist on wine and even a few who say nothing but champagne will do. I would not, however, recommend champagne or any drink with bubbles, including the sweet carbonated drinks. If the food is hot these tend to exaggerate the burning sensation. Dry red wines or fine white wines lose out too in the company of strong spices. You can serve a semi-sweet white wine, a fruity rosé, a fruit and wine punch or chilled beer. I really think though, that a sweet drink such as rose-flavoured sherbet or a glass of *falooda* is far and away the best.

An Indian banquet is a wonderful way to entertain. It is unusual and exotic and provides a talking point. But that is not its chief advantage. The fact is that many Indian dishes, particularly those with meat or poultry as the main ingredient, may be prepared a few days before as they actually improve with being kept – under refrigeration, of course. So for the busy hostess, most of the cooking may be done and out of the way before the day when guests are expected.

Imagine the impact of serving and eating the Indian way – sitting on the floor (on Indian carpets, perhaps) with cushions in brilliant Indian colours to recline on – and eating with the fingers. Try it.

Your guests will love the experience, and somehow the food tastes better. A visiting potentate was so impressed by the custom that he is credited with the remark that eating with spoon and fork is like making love through an interpreter!

With the meal everything is brought on at once – no separate courses to keep the hostess on her feet.

Of course, to be completely authentic, the hostess does not sit and eat with the guests. In Indian homes the womenfolk of the family pamper the guests, attending to their every need, and it is only when they have finished their meal that the women will eat. I am not, however, suggesting that Western hostesses should adopt this custom.

Sitting on the floor or at a table, eating with fingers or forks, Indian food is worth experiencing. Far better to cook it at home from reliable recipes than to eat at restaurants where too often the food is disappointing. The suggestions I have made for dishes to be served together need not be rigidly followed but present ideas you can adapt to your own and your guests' preferences. Happy hostessing!

Guide to Weights and Measures

In all recipes, imperial equivalents of metric measures are shown in parentheses, e.g. 500 g (1 lb) beef. Although the metric yields of cup and weighed measures are approximately 10 per cent greater than the imperial yields, the proportions remain the same. Therefore, for successful cooking use either metric or imperial weights and measures – do not mix the two.

All cup and spoon measurements are level:
- The British Standard measuring cup has a capacity of 250 millilitres (250 ml).
- The British Standard tablespoon has a capacity of 20 millilitres (20 ml).
- The British Standard teaspoon has a capacity of 5 millilitres (5 ml).

Imperial Liquid Measures	Cup Measures	Metric Liquid Measures	Imperial Weight	Metric Weight
1 fl oz		30 ml	½ oz	15 g
2 fl oz	¼ cup		1 oz	30 g
3 fl oz		100 ml	2 oz	60 g
4 fl oz (¼ pint US)	½ cup		3 oz	90 g
5 fl oz (¼ pint imp)		150 ml	4 oz (¼ lb)	125 g
6 fl oz	¾ cup		6 oz	185 g
8 fl oz (½ pint US)	1 cup	250 ml	8 oz (½ lb)	250 g
10 fl oz (½ pint imp)	1¼ cups		12 oz (¾ lb)	375 g
12 fl oz	1½ cups		16 oz (1 lb)	500 g
14 fl oz	1¾ cups		24 oz (1½ lb)	750 g
16 fl oz (1 pint US)	2 cups	500 ml	32 oz (2 lb)	1000 g (1 kg)
20 fl oz (1 pint imp)	2½ cups		3 lb	1500 g (1.5 kg)
32 fl oz	4 cups	1 litre	4 lb	2000 g (2 kg)

Key: fl oz = fluid ounce; ml = millilitre; oz = ounce; lb = pound; g = gram; kg = kilogram.

OVEN TEMPERATURE GUIDE

The Celsius and Fahrenheit temperatures in the chart below relate to most gas ovens. Increase by 20°C or 50°F for electric ovens or refer to the manufacturer's temperature guide. For temperatures below 160°C (325°F), do not increase the given temperature.

Description of oven	Celsius °C	Fahrenheit °F	Gas Mark
Cool	100	200	$\frac{1}{4}$
Very Slow	120	250	$\frac{1}{2}$
Slow	150	300	2
Moderately Slow	160	325	3
Moderate	180	350	4
Moderately Hot	190	375	5
Hot	200	400	6
Very Hot	230	450	8

Appetisers and Snacks

Savoury snacks have a great importance in India. There are so many varieties that it would be impossible to name them all, let alone include the recipes. They range from simple to quite elaborate, from something you would buy in a twist of paper in the market place to a delicacy that has taken hours to prepare.

Snacks are most often served at morning or afternoon tea time in India, instead of cakes and biscuits. Children coming home from school expect to find a snack waiting for them and these are generally savoury rather than sweet. Most are based on lentils, lentil flour or *atta* (wholemeal flour). For instance, *moong dhal*, split peas or *channa dhal* may be soaked to tenderise them, then well drained, dried and deep fried. Add a sprinkle of spices and salt and they make a crisp, nutty titbit.

The immensely popular *sev* is a simple lentil flour dough, judiciously spiced, and pressed through a mould into hot oil. The fine strands like noodles are served on their own or combined with other ingredients for more elaborate snacks. *Nimki* is fried pastry with seeds and spices, *murukku* is similar to *sev* but made with rice flour and shaped in thicker strands, *chiura* is a mixture of flaked rice crisp fried and seasoned with ground spices. *Chiura* is made with flaked rice which is sometimes available in Indian grocery shops, but unsweetened breakfast cereal (corn flakes for instance) makes a very acceptable substitute. Roasted chick peas used in the recipe are available at Greek delicatessen and grocery shops.

More substantial are *samosas* which are pastry turnovers with meat, fish or vegetable fillings. *Pakorhas* are crisp vegetable fritters and they should be eaten immediately they are cooked. They may be just slices of vegetable dipped in lentil flour batter or more elaborate mixtures of vegetables.

Snacks like *thosai* can make a meal. My favourite is the paper *thosai*, literally as thin as paper and crisp as a wafer. Having watched them being made in a vegetarian reтаurant in Karnataka, I saw that nothing less than sleight of hand is required to spread the butter rapidly on the griddle and I suspect that years of practice go into the making of a perfect paper *thosai*. The simple pancake-like *thosai* that the housewife makes is, however, just as flavoursome and when filled with potato masala (*sukhe alu*, page 49), is enough to send homesick Indians into raptures.

The smaller snacks are ideal for serving at cocktail time. At your next party serve the *machchi koftas* or *keema samosas* and wait for the compliments from your guests.

Chiura
Savoury Rice Flakes (Uttar Pradesh)   *Makes about 6 cups*

½ cup oil
1 cup raw peanuts
1 cup roasted chick peas
3 dried red chillies, broken into pieces and seeded
1 teaspoon black mustard seeds
1 teaspoon garam masala (page xxx)

1 teaspoon salt
½ teaspoon chilli powder
2 teaspoons ground cummin
1 teaspoon amchur, optional
4 cups rice flakes (powva)
1 cup potato crisps, optional

In a large karahi or saucepan heat the oil and fry the peanuts until golden brown, stirring constantly. Do not let them darken too much as they will continue to cook in their own heat for a while even when out of the pan. Remove with slotted spoon and drain on absorbent paper. In the oil left in pan toss the roasted chick peas briefly and remove from pan. If necessary add a tablespoon or two of oil to the pan and fry the chillies and mustard seeds until the seeds start to pop. Turn off heat, add the garam masala, salt, chilli powder, cummin, amchur, if used, and mix well. Add the rice flakes and toss well to distribute salt and spices. Taste for seasoning and add extra salt and chilli powder if necessary. Stir in potato crisps, peanuts and chick peas. Cool and store in an airtight container.

Murukku
Rice Flour Crisps (South India)   *Serves: 6–8*

1½ cups rice flour
4 tablespoons besan (chick pea flour)
2½ teaspoons salt
2 teaspoons cummin seeds
1 teaspoon chilli powder or to taste

½ teaspoon ajowan seeds, optional
2 tablespoons ghee
½ cup thick coconut milk (page xxxv)
oil for deep frying

Combine rice flour and besan with all the dry ingredients. Rub the ghee into the flour until evenly distributed, then add enough coconut milk to form a soft dough. Heat oil and force dough into oil in circles through a forcing bag using a star icing nozzle. Fry a few at a time on medium heat until golden brown and crisp, lift out and drain on absorbent paper. Serve warm or cool completely and store in an airtight container. Serve as a snack or cocktail savoury.

Nimki
Fried Pastry Titbits   *Serves: 6–8*

2 cups plain flour
1 teaspoon salt
½ teaspoon chilli powder
½ teaspoon ground cummin
½ teaspoon ajowan seeds
1 teaspoon black cummin seeds

1 teaspoon garam masala
   (page xxx)
3 tablespoons melted ghee
approximately ¼ cup cold water
oil for deep frying

These delicious savouries may be prepared and kept for quite some time in an airtight container. Serve at tea time or with drinks.

Sift flour and salt, chilli powder and ground cummin, into a bowl. Stir the ajowan seeds, black cummin seeds and garam masala through. Rub the melted ghee into the flour, then add enough cold water to mix to a firm dough and knead for 10 minutes or until it is smooth and elastic. Cover and leave aside for 30 minutes.

Roll out small portions of the dough on a lightly floured board until very thin. Cut into finger-size strips and fry a few at a time in hot oil until golden. Drain on absorbent paper. Serve warm, or allow to get quite cold and store in an airtight container. If liked, more salt and garam masala may be sprinkled over the strips before serving.

Channa Dhal
Crisp Fried Split Peas   *Makes approximately 2 cups*

1 cup channa dhal (page 62) or
   yellow split peas (mattar ki
   dhal)
2 teaspoons bicarbonate of soda
oil for deep frying

½ teaspoon chilli powder or to
   taste
½ teaspoon garam masala
   (page xxx)
1 teaspoon salt

A popular snack all over India.

Wash the peas in cold water, then soak overnight in water to cover with the bicarbonate of soda. Drain in a colander, rinse in fresh water and drain once more. After the peas have drained for at least 30 minutes, turn them onto paper towels, spread them out and leave to dry.

Heat oil in a deep frying pan and fry about ½ cup of split peas at a time on medium heat until they are golden. Lift out on slotted spoon and drain on absorbent paper. Repeat until all the peas are fried, then toss them in a mixture of the chilli powder, garam masala and salt. Leave to get quite cold before storing in an airtight container.

Uppuma
Savoury Semolina (South India)   *Serves: 4*

4½ tablespoons vegetable oil
2 cups semolina
1 teaspoon black mustard seeds
8-10 curry leaves
1 tablespoon urad dhal
1 tablespoon channa dhal
4 dried red chillies
1½ cups finely chopped onion
1 tablespoon sliced fresh red or
   green chillies

1 tablespoon grated fresh ginger
1½ cups diced vegetables
   (peppers, peas, carrots,
   cauliflower)
2 cups hot water
1½ teaspoon salt
2 teaspoons ghee
squeeze of lemon juice

Uppuma is a popular snack and may also be served as a breakfast dish.

In a saucepan heat 1½ tablespoons oil and fry the semolina, stirring constantly, until golden. Remove the semolina from pan, wipe out pan with absorbent paper. Heat remaining 3 tablespoons oil in pan and fry the mustard seeds, curry leaves, urad and channa dhals and the dried chillies, broken into pieces. (If a hot result is not desired, shake out and discard the seeds and only use one or two chillies.)

When dhals are golden add onions and fry, stirring, until they are soft and pale golden. Add fresh chillies, ginger and vegetables, stir and cook for about 8 minutes. Add water and salt, bring to the boil, add semolina and stir constantly until it boils. Keep stirring until quite dry. Cover pan tightly and allow to cook on very low heat until semolina is cooked through. Add the ghee and stir it through. Add a squeeze of lemon juice and serve warm or cold. Serve uppuma in small bowls with a spoon for eating.

Machchi Kofta
Fish Balls with Sesame (Bengal)   *Makes about 24*

2 cups flaked cooked fish
1 teaspoon finely grated fresh
   ginger
½ teaspoon crushed garlic or
   garlic powder
¼ teaspoon ground cummin
⅛ teaspoon chilli powder or
   to taste
¾ teaspoon salt

¼ teaspoon ground black pepper
1 small onion, finely chopped
2 tablespoons chopped fresh
   coriander, optional
1 egg, separated
1 tablespoon yoghurt
2 tablespoons sesame seeds
4 tablespoons dry breadcrumbs
oil for deep frying

Leftover curried fish is ideal for this, or any cooked fish will do. (If using curried fish, mix a little of the gravy into the fish for extra flavour.) Carefully remove all skin and bones and mix the flaked fish with the ginger, garlic, cummin, chilli, salt, pepper, onion, coriander (if used), yolk of the egg and the yoghurt. If the fish is very moist, the yoghurt may not be necessary, and in fact it may be replaced with a tablespoon or two of soft breadcrumbs. Use your discretion about this, depending on the fish used. The mixture should be of a good moulding consistency.

Form into small balls and roll these first in the slightly beaten egg white, then in the sesame seeds and breadcrumbs mixed together. Deep fry in hot oil until golden brown. Drain on absorbent paper and serve warm.

Namkin Boondi
Savoury Batter Drops (Punjab)   Serves: 6

1 cup besan (chick pea flour)
1 cup self-raising flour
½ teaspoon cummin seeds
1 teaspoon chilli powder or to taste
1 teaspoon garam masala (page xxx)

½ teaspoon ground turmeric
½ teaspoon crushed garlic or garlic powder
½ teaspoon ajowan seeds
1½ teaspoons salt
approximately 1½ cups tepid water
oil for deep frying
2 tablespoons ghee, optional

Sift the besan and self-raising flours into a bowl. Roast cummin seeds in a dry pan, shaking or stirring constantly until brown, then crush. Stir the cummin seeds, chilli powder, garam masala, turmeric, garlic, ajowan seeds, salt and water into the flour mixture and mix to a smooth, rather thin batter. Heat oil in a karahi or frying pan and, if liked, flavour it with ghee. When oil is smoking hot, hold a perforated spoon over it and pour a spoonful of the batter onto the spoon. Tap the handle against the side of the pan so that drops of the batter fall into the oil. Cook only one spoonful at a time. As the drops swell and turn golden brown, lift them out with another frying spoon and drain on absorbent paper. Repeat in the same way until all the batter is used up. The namkin boondi may be stored, when cool, in an airtight container. Serve as a savoury with drinks, or as a tea-time nibble.

Note: The perforations in the spoon should be round and about the size of a pea. The batter should be of a medium pouring consistency. A thick batter will result in more even shapes, but the drops will not be as delightfully crisp as with a thin batter.

Alu Mattar Samosa
Potato and Pea Pastries   Makes about 36

500 g (1 lb) potatoes
¾ cup fresh or frozen peas
1 teaspoon salt
1 teaspoon ground cummin
½ teaspoon chilli powder, optional

½ teaspoon panch phora (page xxxi)
2 tablespoons lemon juice
1 quantity pastry as for keema samosa (page 8)
oil for deep frying

Prepare pastry and set aside while preparing filling. Boil the potatoes, peel and dice. If using fresh peas, cook them until tender. Frozen peas need only to be thawed. Combine potatoes and peas with the salt, cummin, chilli powder (if used), panch phora and lemon juice and make up samosas using method described for keema samosa (page 8). Deep fry in hot oil. Drain on absorbent paper and serve warm or cold.

Jhinga Samosa
Prawn Pastries (Bengal)   *Makes about 30*

500 g (1 lb) raw prawns
250 g (8 oz) potatoes
2 tablespoons ghee or oil
2 medium onions, finely
   chopped
1 teaspoon chopped garlic
1 teaspoon finely grated fresh
   ginger

½ teaspoon ground turmeric
½ teaspoon chilli powder
1 teaspoon salt or to taste
¼ cup hot water
lemon juice to taste
1 quantity pastry as for keema
   samosa (see page 8), or
   frozen spring roll wrappers
oil for deep frying

Shell and de-vein the prawns and chop into large pieces. Peel and cut the potatoes into pieces the same size as the prawns. Heat the ghee or oil and fry the onions, garlic and ginger until onions are soft and golden. Add turmeric and chilli powder, the prawns and potatoes. Stir well, add salt and about ¼ cup hot water, cover and cook until potatoes are tender. Remove from heat, add lemon juice to taste and allow to cool before enclosing in pastry or strips of spring roll wrappers as described for keema samosa (page 8).

Heat oil for deep drying and fry until crisp and golden. Drain on absorbent paper.

Keema Samosa
Meat Filled Pastries (North India)   *Makes about 36*

Pastry:
1½ cups plain flour
¾ teaspoon salt
1 tablespoon ghee or oil
½ cup warm water

Filling:
1 tablespoon oil or ghee
2 medium onions, finely chopped
1 fresh red or green chilli, seeded and chopped
½ teaspoon crushed garlic
2 teaspoons finely chopped fresh ginger
1 teaspoon ground coriander
1 teaspoon ground cummin
½ teaspoon ground turmeric
½ teaspoon chilli powder, optional
½ teaspoon salt or to taste
1 tablespoon lemon juice
250 g (8 oz) minced lamb
½ cup hot water
½ teaspoon garam masala (page xxx)
2 tablespoons chopped fresh mint or coriander leaves
oil for deep frying

Pastry: Sift flour and salt into a bowl, lightly rub in ghee or oil, add warm water and mix until ingredients are combined and the dough comes away from side of bowl. Add a little more water if necessary. Knead firmly for 10 minutes or until dough is smooth and elastic. Cover with plastic wrap and set aside for at least 30 minutes, while preparing filling.

Filling: Heat oil or ghee in a saucepan and fry half the chopped onion and fresh chilli until soft, then add garlic and half the ginger and continue to fry, stirring, until it starts to brown. Add coriander, cummin, turmeric and chilli powder (if used) and fry for a few seconds longer. Add salt and lemon juice. Add meat and fry over high heat, stirring constantly, until meat changes colour. Lower heat and add hot water, cover pan and cook until meat is tender and all the liquid has been absorbed, about 25 minutes. Stir frequently towards end of cooking, when mixture is dry. Stir in the garam masala and allow mixture to cool. Mix in the chopped herbs and remaining chopped onion and ginger, which get half cooked during frying, giving good texture and extra flavour to the filling.

Make small balls of dough and roll out each one on a lightly floured board to the size of a saucer. Dough should be fairly thin. Cut each circle of dough in half. Put a teaspoon of filling on one side of each half circle, brush edges with water, fold dough over and press edges together firmly to seal. The samosas should be triangular.

When all the samosas are made, heat oil in a deep pan and fry a few at a time on medium high heat, spooning the oil over the tops. Fry until golden brown on both sides. Drain on absorbent paper and serve hot. These samosas are sometimes accompanied by podina chatni (page 139) or imli chatni (page 141), for dipping.

Note: A quick and easy method is to use frozen spring roll pastry. Buy the large size pastry squares, thaw the packet and carefully peel away 12 sheets. Wrap the remainder and return to freezer. This pastry keeps well. Cut each sheet into three equal strips and keep them covered while working or they will dry out. Put 1 teaspoon of filling at one end and fold the strip of pastry over diagonally, then fold again and again, making sure there is a perfect triangle every time. Moisten end of strip with water or a mixture of beaten egg and flour to seal. Fry as above.

Pakorhas
Vegetable Fritters   *Makes about 36*

¾ cup besan (chick pea flour)
¾ cup self-raising flour
1½ teaspoons crushed garlic
1½ teaspoons salt
1 teaspoon garam masala
  (page xxx)
½ teaspoon chilli powder,
  optional

approximately 1 cup water
2 medium potatoes
1 medium eggplant
2 medium onions
few tender spinach leaves
oil for deep frying

Combine besan and self-raising flour with garlic, salt, garam masala, chilli powder and water. Beat until smooth and light. It should be of a thin coating consistency. Cover bowl and set aside for 1 hour or longer. Meanwhile, prepare the vegetables.

Peel the potatoes and cut in very thin round slices. Soak in cold water. Do not peel the eggplant but slice thinly and, if large, cut into bite-size pieces. Peel the onions and cut in halves lengthways, then cut in thin slices, leaving a bit of the root end on each slice to hold the layers of onion together. Wash and dry spinach leaves and tear into pieces.

Heat oil in karahi or frying pan. Dip individual pieces of vegetable in the batter, allow any excess to drip off, and immerse in the hot oil. Do not fry too many at a time or the temperature of the oil will drop, resulting in tough, oily pakorhas. They should be feather-light and crisp. Drain on absorbent paper and serve warm with a fresh chutney such as imli chatni (page 141) or podina chatni (page 139) for dipping.

Thosai
Lentil and Rice Pancakes (South India)　　　　　*Makes about 18*

1½ cups uncooked rice
¾ cup urad dhal (page 62)
2 teaspoons salt
1½ teaspoons sugar
2 teaspoons ghee or oil

½ teaspoon black mustard seeds
1 small onion, finely chopped
1 fresh green chilli, seeded and
　chopped

Wash rice and urad dhal separately and soak each in cold water to cover for 8 hours. Drain and grind rice in electric blender, adding just enough water to facilitate blending. Strain through a fine sieve and discard rough residue, if any.

Rinse blender and grind the urad dhal, adding a little cold water as necessary. This should not need straining, as urad dhal blends more easily than rice. Combine urad dhal and rice and mix well, adding salt and sugar. Cover and leave to ferment in a warm place for 2 or 3 hours.

Heat ghee or oil in small saucepan and fry the mustard seeds until they pop. Add onion and chilli and fry, stirring now and then, until the onions start to colour. Remove from heat and when cool stir into the batter. The batter should be of a thick pouring consistency. Thin it down if necessary with a little cold water.

Heat a tawa, heavy frying pan or pancake pan and grease with very little ghee or oil. Pour in about ⅓ cup of batter, or just enough to cover base of pan thinly. The trick is to spread the batter very quickly with the back of the ladle or metal cup used for pouring. Allow to cook on low heat until the bottom is well browned. Turn over and cook other side. Serve with nariyal chatni (page 140) and a vegetable preparation such as sukhe alu (page 49) or alu mattar bhaji (page 52).

Rice and Bread

Rice or bread is almost always served as a background to Indian meals. Their very neutrality makes them ideal accompaniments to spicy dishes as well as counteracting the after-effects of a rich, highly seasoned meal. In Asia the grain is treated with respect and even reverence.

RICE

Rice is, without a doubt, the most important cereal crop in the world and is the staple food of more than half the world's population.

Of all the land under cultivation in India, a quarter is given to rice. It is an indispensable part of every meal in southern and eastern parts of India and no matter what else is on the table, rice has pride of place. Even in the north and central regions where chapatis and naan are eaten, rice still features strongly, especially in festive pilaus and birianis.

There are records going back over five thousand years telling of the cultivation of rice in India and China. This ancient and honourable grain is treated with respect and reverence, for in Asia the failure of a rice crop is no mere economic setback – it casts the ugly shadow of famine. Small wonder then, that those who live in Asia are reluctant to waste even the smallest amount of rice. The feeling that not even a grain should be thrown away amounts almost to superstition.

In areas where rice is grown and eaten in preference to wheat, it is eaten at least twice a day, yet it is never boring as there is such an infinite variety of ways of preparing it and combining it with grains, lentils, vegetables, meat, poultry or fish. Rice also features prominently in the sweet dishes cooked during religious festivities and it is considered a symbol of plenty.

Different types of rice are particularly suited to different kinds of dishes. Long grain rice, especially the thin, fine grains of basmati, are prized for pilau and biriani while medium and short grain rice is preferred for creamy rice and milk sweets.

Since there are so many millions of people who depend on rice and eat it every day, naturally enough there are many different ways of cooking it. Some cooks wash the rice several times, while others would not dream of doing this, believing that valuable nutrients would be lost. Other cooks soak the rice for a time before cooking. Each method works when carried out properly.

Most experienced cooks put the rice into the pot, add enough cold water to come to the knuckle of the middle finger held at right angles to the rice. This gives perfect, separate grains by the absorption method to the regular and practised cook who uses the right size pot, the right degree of heat and cooks it for the right length of time. The amateur, when it comes to rice cooking, needs rather more precise rules, and this is what I have given in the individual recipes and in the table that follows.

In Asia one finds there is usually a pot used just for boiling rice. The cook knows exactly how much water to add to the rice in that particular pot to get a perfect result every time. I have found the following table works for me, no matter if I am cooking rice for two or for twenty-two. It works irrespective of the size of the pot and even if left to cook longer than it should have been . . . well, not *too* much longer. The only requisite is a well-fitting lid to keep the steam in, for it is the steam that cooks the rice. A good, heavy-based pan helps too but if your pan is rather light be sure to turn the heat down low so that the rice does not burn.

Soaking the rice in cold water seems to improve the yield when it is cooked, and gives longer, more separate grains. In individual recipes I have adjusted the amount of liquid accordingly.

If rice must be fried before liquid is added, the washed rice must be given enough time to drain and dry thoroughly, from 30-60 minutes depending on the quantity of rice and the method of draining. A large colander or sieve with plenty of surface area naturally helps the drying.

Rice to be cooked by the absorption method, put straight into water without previously being fried, may be washed if necessary, drained briefly and added to the pot immediately. If the rice retains much water and there is no time for draining, reduce the measure of water by about $\frac{1}{4}$ cup for every 4 cups water required.

SHORT OR MEDIUM GRAIN RICE
Allow $1\frac{1}{2}$ cups water for the first cup of rice and 1 cup water for each additional cup of rice.

1 cup rice	$1\frac{1}{2}$ cups water
2 cups rice	$2\frac{1}{2}$ cups water
3 cups rice	$3\frac{1}{2}$ cups water

For each cup of rice, add 1 level teaspoon salt to the water. Bring rice and water to a bubbling boil over high heat, then turn heat very low, cover pan tightly with well fitting lid and cook for 20 minutes. Remove from heat, uncover pan and let steam escape for a few minutes before fluffing rice with fork. Transfer rice to serving dish with a slotted metal spoon – wooden spoons or similar utensils crush the grains.

You will notice that long grain rice absorbs considerably more water so the type of rice stipulated in a recipe should not be changed unless the amount of water is adjusted.

LONG GRAIN RICE
2 cups water for the first cup of rice, plus 1½ cups water for each additional cup of rice.

1 cup rice	2 cups water
2 cups rice	3½ cups water
3 cups rice	5 cups water

If, however, you are cooking a really large quantity of rice, do not increase the water at the same rate. Start reducing liquid from 8 cups rice onwards. Up to this point the above proportions work very well, but after this cut down slightly:

8 cups rice	12 cups water (not 12½)
9 cups rice	13 cups water

and then increase by 1 cup water to each cup of rice.

It is doubtful you will have to cook in such quantities very often, but just in case, it is useful to know.

NATURAL OR UNPOLISHED RICE
This is rice that has been husked but not polished to remove the bran. It is more nutritious than polished rice and I would like to see it being used more often, though it has a much more chewy texture and is not really favoured in India. With the new health conscious approach to eating I anticipate that people will be prepared to sacrifice some of the qualities of polished rice, if not for special occasions at least for family meals. Any of the recipes in this chapter may be adapted to use natural rice. Use the same proportions of water as for long grain rice but allow 15-20 minutes more cooking time as the bran coating of the grains makes absorption much slower. The flavour, however, will be just as delicious.

BREAD

Bread, that most basic of foods, is a fascinating subject. All over the world breads are made from the same basic ingredients – grain, water and salt – yet they have tremendous individuality. At the same time there are striking similarities. The *chapati* of India, the *tortilla* of Mexico and the *pita* of the Middle East, all flat, round loaves, are first cousins for sure.

The bread in Tashkent in Soviet Central Asia is almost identical to the morning bread in Kashmir in the Himalayas – round loaves with an indentation in the centre bearing a distinctive pattern formed by intersecting lines.

Rumali roti, an Indian bread, and *shrak*, bread of the Bedouins, are again so similar as to make one wonder how the similarity came about. Both are paper thin and as large as a bicycle wheel and both are cooked on a convex griddle.

To make Indian bread is easy and much quicker than it is to make the leavened breads of the West. Since most of the breads are made from whole grains, there is the added advantage of good nutrition.

In north and central India, wheat is the most commonly used grain and whole wheat flour called *atta* is the basic ingredient in many of the breads. Maize, millet, sorghum, lentils and even rice are also used, but wheat is the most popular.

Chapatis made from atta and cooked on an ungreased *tawa* or griddle are eaten at breakfast, lunch and dinner. *Parathas* are also made from *atta* but are rich and flaky because they have been spread with ghee and folded in a special way so that they are somewhat like flaky pastry. They are shallow fried, on a griddle lightly greased with ghee, and more melted ghee is drizzled on top of them as they cook. *Puris* are smaller and are deep fried so they puff like balloons. These breads are all unleavened. Then there are those breads that do have leavening and therefore take longer to make, such as *naan* and *bhatura*.

Naan is a yeast-risen white flour bread with yoghurt, egg and butter. *Bhatura* is a sour dough bread using whole wheat flour. *Bhatura* is deep fried while *naan* is baked in the *tandoor*, the dough shaped with a few expert pats between skilled hands, then placed on a cloth pad and slapped against the white-hot sides of the earthen oven through the small opening at the top.

I watched a stalwart, bearded Sikh tend a *tandoor*, so completely in control that he was turning out almost simultaneously *tandoori* chicken, *tikka kebab*, *seekh kebab* and a never-ending supply of *naan* and *tandoori roti*.

It is even more fascinating to watch *rumali roti* being made. The name means that it is as thin as a silken scarf and while this may be a touch of poetic licence, it is a truly fine bread which is not rolled to achieve its thinness, but rather flung in the air. Those who have watched it done will be reminded of flamboyant pizza makers or those nimble-fingered hawkers in Singapore and Malaysia who make *murtaba*.

There are breads with fillings of meat, vegetables, lentils or cheese but it is the humble *chapati*, eaten with yoghurt, lentils and cooked greens of various types known as *saag*, that is literally the daily bread of millions of Indians.

Namkin Chawal

Plain Savoury Rice   *Serves: 4–6*

2½ cups long grain rice	2 teaspoons ghee
4 cups hot water	2½ teaspoons salt

Rice is the staple food in southern, central and eastern parts of India and when eaten at an Indian meal forms the major part of the meal. Served Indian-style, this quantity will serve four.

Wash rice well and soak 1 hour in cold water. Drain in colander while bringing water, ghee and salt to the boil in a heavy saucepan with a well-fitting lid. Add rice, stir and bring quickly to the boil. Turn heat very low, cover tightly and cook, without lifting lid or stirring, for 20–25 minutes. Lift lid to allow steam to escape for about 5 minutes, then lightly fluff up rice with fork, taking care not to mash the grains, which will be firm, separate and perfectly cooked. Dish up using a slotted metal spoon rather than a wooden spoon, which will crush the grains. Serve with curries or other spiced dishes.

Pilau

Rice Cooked in Stock (Uttar Pradesh)   *Serves: 4–6*

1 x 1 kg (2 lb) chicken or
  3 lamb shanks
4 cardamom pods, bruised
10 whole black peppercorns
4½ teaspoons salt
1 onion stuck with 3 whole
  cloves
2½ cups long grain rice
5 tablespoons ghee
1 large onion, finely sliced
¼ teaspoon saffron strands or
  ⅛ teaspoon powdered saffron
1 teaspoon crushed garlic
½ teaspoon finely grated
  fresh ginger
½ teaspoon garam masala
  (page xxx)
½ teaspoon ground cardamom
3 tablespoons rose water
¼ cup sultanas

Garnish:
¼ cup fried almonds
1 cup hot cooked green peas
3 hard-boiled eggs, halved

Make a strong, well-flavoured stock by simmering chicken or lamb in water to cover, with cardamom pods, peppercorns, 2 teaspoons salt and the onion stuck with cloves. Simmer for approximately 2 hours. Cool slightly, strain stock and measure 4 cups. Remove meat from bones, cut into bite-size pieces and set aside.

Wash rice thoroughly in water, drain in a colander and allow to dry for at least 30 minutes. Heat ghee in a large saucepan and fry sliced onion until golden. If using saffron strands, grind with pestle and mortar and dissolve in 1 tablespoon hot water. Add saffron, garlic and ginger and fry for 1 minute, stirring constantly. Add rice and fry 5 minutes longer over a moderate heat, stirring with a slotted metal spoon. (This prevents breaking the long delicate grains of rice which add so much to the appearance of this dish.) Add 4 cups hot stock, garam masala, cardamom, remaining salt, rose water, sultanas and reserved chicken or lamb pieces, stir well. Cover pan with a tightly fitting lid and cook over a very low heat for 20 minutes.

Do not uncover saucepan or stir rice during cooking time.

When rice is cooked, remove from heat and stand, uncovered, for 5 minutes. Fluff up rice gently with a fork and place in a dish, again using a slotted metal spoon. Garnish with almonds, peas and eggs and serve hot accompanied by curry, khira raita (page 136), pickles and crisp fried pappadams.

Rajasthani Pilau
Festive Spiced Rice (Rajasthan)   *Serves: 6*

2½ cups long grain rice
3 tablespoons ghee or oil
2 medium onions, finely sliced
2 sticks cinnamon
6 cardamom pods, bruised
6 whole cloves
4 cups hot stock or water
2½ teaspoons salt

Garnish:
red and green food colouring
carrots and tomatoes

The State of Rajasthan is beautiful. Costumes in vivid colours dazzle and enchant. Even the food reflects this love of colour, dishes being garnished with the bright reds and greens that Rajasthani folk delight in.

If the rice needs washing, wash well in several changes of cold water and leave to soak for 1 hour. Then drain in a colander for at least 30 minutes.

Heat ghee or oil in a large, heavy saucepan and fry the sliced onion with the cinnamon, cardamoms and cloves until the onions are golden, stirring frequently so that they brown evenly. Add the rice and fry for about 3 minutes, then pour in the stock or water. Add the salt and stir well while bringing quickly to the boil. Turn heat very low, cover tightly and cook without lifting lid for 25 minutes. Uncover, allow steam to escape for a few minutes, remove whole spices.

Take ½ cup cooked rice and colour bright red; colour an equal amount bright green. Garnish the dish with tomato and carrot roses and the coloured rice. Serve hot with mutton sula (page 113).

Navrattan Pilau

Rice with Fresh Cheese, Nuts and   *Serves: 6*
Vegetables (Moghul Style)

2½ cups basmati rice or other
   long grain rice
250 g (8 oz) panir or ricotta
   cheese (page xxiii)
oil for deep frying
2 tablespoons ghee
1 teaspoon ground turmeric
1 cup hot water
¼ cup slivered blanched
   almonds
2 medium onions, thinly sliced
1 teaspoon finely chopped garlic
2 teaspoons finely shredded
   fresh ginger
5 cardamom pods, bruised
1 small stick cinnamon
3 whole cloves
10 whole black peppercorns
1 cup small cauliflower sprigs
½ cup shelled peas
4 cups water
3 teaspoons salt
2 tablespoons pistachio kernels,
   blanched (page xxiv)
¼ cup sultanas

Garnish:
small red tomatoes

Navrattan means 'nine jewels', as the nine courtiers of Emperor Akbar were called.

Wash rice well and leave to drain for at least 30 minutes. Cut ricotta cheese or panir into small cubes and leave on absorbent paper to drain if there is any excess moisture. In a heavy saucepan heat enough oil to deep fry the cubes of cheese, and add to it 1 tablespoon of the ghee to flavour it. Have ready the ground turmeric stirred into a cup of hot water. Deep fry the cubes of cheese, a few at a time, until just golden. Remove from oil with slotted spoon and soak in the turmeric water. When all have been fried and soaked for 5 minutes, remove them to kitchen paper to drain. In the same oil fry the almonds until golden, remove and drain.

Pour off all but about 2 tablespoons oil, add the remaining tablespoon of ghee and fry the sliced onions, garlic, ginger, cardamom, cinnamon, cloves and peppercorns. When the onions are golden add the cauliflower and peas and fry for 2 minutes, then add the rice and fry, stirring, for a further 3 minutes. Add water and salt, bring to the boil, then turn heat very low and cook, tightly covered, for 20 minutes without lifting lid or stirring. Remove from heat, pick out whole spices which will have come to the top. Fork the fried cheese, half the almonds, pistachios and sultanas through the rice. Dish up and garnish with remaining nuts and sultanas and small red tomatoes. Serve with a rich meat curry such as roghan josh (page 118) or kofta kari (page 133).

Mattar Pilau

Rice with Fresh Peas (Uttar Pradesh)   *Serves: 4–5*

1½ cups long grain rice	1 teaspoon cummin seeds
1 tablespoon ghee	½ teaspoon ground turmeric
4 whole cloves	1½ cups shelled green peas
1 small cinnamon stick	2½ teaspoons salt
3 or 4 cardamom pods, bruised	3¼ cups hot water

Wash the rice well and leave to soak in cold water for 30 minutes, then drain well. Heat the ghee in a heavy saucepan and fry the cloves, cinnamon, cardamom pods and cummin seeds, for 1 minute. Add turmeric and rice and stir over medium heat for about 3 minutes. Add peas, salt and hot water. Bring quickly to the boil, then turn heat very low, cover with a well-fitting lid and cook for 25–30 minutes without lifting lid or stirring. Uncover at end of cooking time to allow steam to escape for about 3 minutes. Remove whole spices, fork rice grains lightly and serve hot with meat or vegetable curries.

Moglai Murgh Pilau

Spiced Rice with Chicken (Uttar Pradesh)   *Serves: 10–12*

2 x 1.5 kg (3 lb) roasting chickens
8 small new potatoes, optional
6 tablespoons ghee (or half
  ghee, half oil)
4 large onions, finely chopped
1½ tablespoons finely chopped
  garlic
1½ tablespoons finely grated
  fresh ginger
1 teaspoon chilli powder or
  to taste
1 teaspoon ground black
  pepper
1 teaspoon ground turmeric
2 teaspoons ground cummin
3 teaspoons salt
3 large ripe tomatoes, peeled
  and chopped
¾ cup yoghurt
4 tablespoons chopped fresh
  mint
2 or 3 fresh red or green chillies,
  whole
1 teaspoon ground cardamom
1 small cinnamon stick

Pilau Rice:
5 cups basmati or other long
  grain rice
4 tablespoons ghee
2 large onions, finely sliced
½ teaspoon saffron strands or
  ¼ teaspoon powdered saffron
1 tablespoon hot water
10 cardamom pods, bruised
6 whole cloves
1 small cinnamon stick
1 teaspoon ground aromatic
  ginger
4 tablespoons rose water or
  1 teaspoon rose essence
5 teaspoons salt
8 cups hot chicken stock

Garnish:
½ cup sultanas
½ cup split, blanched almonds
ghee for frying
8 hard boiled eggs
1 cup cooked green peas
½ cup coloured rice, optional

*A special dish for a special occasion. For a smaller number of people
halve the quantities but retain the cooking times.*

Cut chickens into serving pieces. Peel and halve the potatoes (if
used). Heat ghee or ghee and oil in a small frying pan and fry the
potatoes until they are brown on the outside. Remove potatoes from
pan with a slotted spoon. Pour the ghee left in frying pan into a large
saucepan, and if there is insufficient to cover base of pan, add a little
more ghee or oil. Heat pan and fry the onions, garlic and ginger until
soft and golden. Add chilli powder, pepper, turmeric, cummin, salt
and tomatoes. Fry, stirring constantly for 5 minutes. Add yoghurt,

mint, chillies, cardamom and cinnamon. Cover and cook over low heat, stirring occasionally, until tomato is cooked to a pulp. (It may be necessary to add a little hot water if mixture becomes too dry and starts sticking to pan.) When thick and smooth, add chicken pieces and stir well to coat them with spice mixture. Cover and cook over very low heat until chicken is tender, about 35–45 minutes. There should be only a very small amount of thick gravy when chicken is cooked. If there is too much gravy, cook uncovered for the last 10–15 minutes to reduce gravy.

Pilau Rice: Wash rice well and drain in colander for at least 30 minutes. Heat ghee in saucepan and fry onion until golden brown. Remove on slotted spoon and set aside. Pound saffron strands in mortar and pestle and dissolve in hot water. Add to ghee together with cardamom pods, cloves, cinnamon stick, aromatic ginger and rice. Fry, stirring constantly until rice is coated with the ghee. Add rose water or essence and salt to hot chicken stock, pour over rice mixture and stir. Add chicken savoury and fried potatoes and gently mix.

Cover saucepan tightly, turn heat very low and cook for 25 minutes without lifting lid or stirring. Serve hot, garnished with the sultanas and almonds fried in ghee, halved hard-boiled eggs, peas and fried onions. For coloured rice, take ½ cup of the cooked rice and colour it a bright orange with a little dissolved saffron or orange food colouring.

Serve this festive dish accompanied by a creamy raita, fresh chutney and a hot Indian pickle.

Bhuna Kitchri
Rice with Mixed Lentils (Uttar Pradesh)   *Serves: 4–5*

1 cup moong dhal (page 62)
½ cup red lentils (masoor dhal –
  page 62)
1½ cups basmati or other
  long grain rice
500 g (1 lb) fresh peas
1 tablespoon ghee
3 tablespoons vegetable oil
6 cardamom pods, bruised
1 small stick cinnamon
4 small bay leaves
4 whole cloves
4 large onions, finely sliced
1 tablespoon finely grated
  fresh ginger
1 fresh green chilli, seeded and
  sliced
½ teaspoon cummin seeds
½ teaspoon ground turmeric
1 teaspoon ground cummin
4 cups hot water
3½ teaspoons salt

Garnish:
2 tablespoons chopped fresh
  coriander, optional

*Allow at least 30 minutes before starting to cook, to prepare lentils
and rice. A nutritious vegetarian meal in one dish.*

In a dry pan roast the moong dhal, stirring constantly, until evenly
brown. Turn into a bowl and wash well, then leave to drain. Wash
red lentils separately and leave to drain. If using basmati rice or
other rice that needs washing, wash well and leave to drain for at
least 30 minutes. Meanwhile, shell the peas. There should be about
¾ cup of shelled peas.

Heat the ghee and oil in a heavy saucepan. Add the cardamom
pods, cinnamon, bay leaves and cloves and the sliced onions. Fry
over medium heat, stirring frequently, until the onions are golden
brown. Remove to a plate with a slotted spoon. To the oil left in the
pan add the ginger, chilli and cummin seeds. Fry, stirring, until

ginger is golden. Add the rice and red lentils and fry, stirring, for 3 minutes. Add the turmeric, ground cummin and fry for a further 2 minutes. Add fresh peas, moong dhal, water and salt, stir and bring to the boil. Return the cardamoms, cinnamon, bay leaves and cloves to the pan. Turn heat very low, cover and cook for 30–35 minutes or until liquid is absorbed and peas tender. Transfer to serving dish with a metal spoon and garnish with the fried onions and the chopped fresh coriander, if used.

Serve with an accompaniment of peeled, diced tomatoes dressed with a pinch of chilli powder and salt to taste. Pickles or chutneys and a bowl of yoghurt complete the meal.

Nariyal Bhath

Rice in Coconut Milk (South India)   *Serves: 6*

2½ cups long grain rice
2 tablespoons ghee
2 medium onions, finely sliced
10 curry leaves
10 whole black peppercorns
1 small stick cinnamon
6 cardamom pods, bruised
6 whole cloves
¾ teaspoon ground turmeric
4 cups coconut milk (page xxxv)
2½ teaspoons salt

Garnish:
½ cup fried cashew nuts

Wash rice and drain for at least 30 minutes. Heat the ghee in a heavy saucepan and fry the onions, curry leaves and whole spices, stirring frequently, until the onions are golden. Add the turmeric and the rice and fry, stirring, until the rice is coated with the ghee, about 3 or 4 minutes. Add the coconut milk and salt, stir and bring to the boil, then cover with a well-fitting lid, turn heat very low and cook for 25 minutes or until the coconut milk is absorbed.

Serve the rice hot, garnished with fried cashews and accompanied by curries and sambals.

Shahjahani Biriani
Layered Rice and Lamb (Uttar Pradesh)   *Serves: 10–12*

2.5 kg (5 lb) leg of lamb, boned
1 medium onion, roughly
   chopped
1 tablespoon chopped fresh
   ginger
2 tablespoons chopped garlic
1 tablespoon white poppy
   seeds, optional
1 or 2 dried red chillies, seeded
   and soaked in hot water
3 tablespoons ground almonds
2 teaspoons ground cummin
½ teaspoon ground cardamom
½ teaspoon ground cinnamon
½ teaspoon ground nutmeg
   or mace
⅛ teaspoon ground cloves
3 tablespoons ghee or oil
3 teaspoons salt
½ cup yoghurt

Rice:
5 cups basmati rice
8 cups water
5 teaspoons salt
2 small sticks cinnamon
8 cardamom pods, bruised
1 teaspoon rose essence
2 drops kewra essence or
   1 teaspoon kewra water,
   optional
½ teaspoon saffron strands
2 tablespoons boiling water
¾ cup pouring cream
little extra ghee or butter
1½ teaspoons black cummin
   seeds

Garnish:
½ cup fried slivered almonds
½ cup fried cashew halves
¼ cup blanched and lightly
   fried pistachios
½ cup sultanas, lightly fried
2 large onions, finely sliced,
   fried golden brown
silver leaf (varak) to decorate

Trim off all excess fat and cut the lean meat into 5 cm (2 inch) cubes.
Put onion, ginger, garlic, poppy seeds (if used) and chillies into
electric blender and blend until all ingredients are finely ground,
adding a little water to facilitate blending. Add the ground almonds
and all the ground spices and blend for a few seconds.

Heat ghee in a large, heavy pan and fry the blended mixture over
medium heat, stirring constantly, until the spices are well cooked
and aromatic and the oil starts to separate from the mass. Wash out
blender jar with ¼ cup water, add to pan and stir until liquid

evaporates again. Add the salt and the cubes of lamb, stirring until each piece is coated with the spices. Lower heat, cover and simmer for 1 hour or until lamb is almost tender. Beat yoghurt with a little water until smooth, add to the pan and cook until almost all the liquid is evaporated and the gravy is very thick.

Rice: While lamb is cooking, wash the rice in several changes of water and leave to soak in cold water for 30 minutes, then drain well. Put rice into a heavy pan with well-fitting lid and add the water, salt, whole spices and the rose and kewra flavourings. Bring quickly to the boil, then turn heat low, cover tightly and cook for 15 minutes without lifting lid. Rice will be almost cooked and the liquid absorbed. Pound the saffron strands in mortar and pestle, dissolve in 1 tablespoon boiling water and stir into the cream. Use second tablespoon of water to rinse out the mortar so that none of the saffron is lost.

In a large, heavy casserole greased with ghee or butter, spread half the rice in an even layer and pour half the cream over. Sprinkle with half the black cummin seeds. Spread with the lamb savoury, taking it right to the edges. Spread remaining rice over the lamb and pour remaining cream over the rice, sprinkle with remaining black cummin seeds.

Cover the dish with aluminium foil and fold the foil carefully over the edge. Flatten the foil by pressing gently with hands and to prevent rice drying out during baking, put 2 or 3 tablespoons water on the foil before covering with lid of dish.

Bake in a moderately slow oven 160°C (325°F) for 40–45 minutes. Serve in the casserole or turn out on a large serving dish and garnish with the fried nuts, sultanas, onions and the silver leaf. The edible silver leaf is made from pure silver and is extremely delicate, so handle it with dry fingertips, holding it between the sheets of thin tissue in which it is packed. Flutter it gently onto the food in a few places for a really festive look to the biriani.

Note: I find it is convenient to heat the ghee needed for frying garnishes in a small frying pan and to fry the various garnishes separately. From what is left measure the ghee needed for cooking the lamb. For a less rich result, use half ghee and half light vegetable oil.

Noor Mahal Biriani
Rice with Lamb and Koftas (Uttar Pradesh)   *Serves: 6*

3 cups basmati or other
  long grain rice
500 g (1 lb) lean lamb
500 g (1 lb) minced lamb
5 teaspoons salt
1 teaspoon garam masala
  (page xxx)
½ teaspoon crushed garlic
4 tablespoons ghee or butter
2 medium onions, finely
  chopped
4 teaspoons finely chopped
  garlic
2 teaspoons finely grated fresh
  ginger
½ cup yoghurt
½ teaspoon paprika
¼ teaspoon ground black
  pepper
¼ teaspoon ground cinnamon
¼ teaspoon ground nutmeg
¼ teaspoon ground cardamom
⅛ teaspoon ground cloves
5 cups hot lamb stock or water

Garnish:
1 cup raw cashews
red, green and yellow food
  colouring
salt to taste
few red cherries, optional

Wash the rice well and soak in cold water for 30 minutes, then drain.
Cut lamb into small cubes. Mix the minced lamb with 1 teaspoon
salt, garam masala and the crushed garlic and form into small koftas
(meatballs).

Heat the ghee or butter in a large, heavy saucepan and fry the
onions, chopped garlic and ginger until golden. Add cubed lamb
and fry, stirring, until colour changes. Stir in yoghurt mixed with a
cup of water, 1 teaspoon salt and the paprika and pepper. Cover and
cook until lamb is half done, then add the koftas and continue
cooking until lamb is tender, stirring occasionally. If there is much
liquid in the pan uncover and cook, stirring, until it is almost all
evaporated.

Now add the rice, the remaining 3 teaspoons salt, the ground spices and stock or water. Bring to the boil, cover with a well-fitting lid, turn heat very low and cook for 25 minutes without lifting lid or stirring, until all the liquid has been absorbed by the rice. Uncover and allow steam to escape for a couple of minutes.

While rice is cooking, boil the cashews in water to which food colouring has been added, and a little salt. Colour some cashews red, some green and some yellow. Ground turmeric may be used for the yellow colouring. Or, if preferred, simply fry the nuts in oil until golden brown. The bright coloured garnish, however, is typical of the love of colour evident in the dress, dwellings and festive dishes of the area.

Serve the rice piping hot, garnished with the nuts, koftas and cherries (if used). A raita, a fresh chutney and a few crisp pappadams are all the accompaniments necessary but for special occasions serve curries as well.

Til Bhath

Rice with Sesame Seeds (South India)   *Serves: 4–6*

2½ cups long grain rice   1 teaspoon mustard seeds
4 cups water   12 curry leaves
2½ teaspoons salt   1 cup sesame seeds
2 tablespoons light sesame oil   lemon juice to taste

Put rice, water and salt into a heavy saucepan, bring to the boil. Cover with well-fitting lid, turn heat very low and cook for 20 minutes. Turn off heat and leave while preparing seasoning.

Heat sesame oil in small saucepan and fry the mustard seeds and curry leaves until leaves are brown and mustard seeds pop. Add the sesame seeds and keep stirring over medium heat until the seeds are evenly golden brown. Mix this seasoning together with the hot cooked rice and add a little lemon juice to taste. Serve with curried vegetables, fresh chutney and fried pappadams.

Moti Pilau

Spiced Rice with Meatballs (Uttar Pradesh)   *Serves: 4*

Meatballs:
500 g (1 lb) minced lamb or beef
1 medium onion, finely
   chopped
1 teaspoon cummin seeds
½ teaspoon crushed garlic
½ teaspoon finely grated
   fresh ginger
1 teaspoon salt
½ teaspoon garam masala
   (page xxx)
2 teaspoons chopped fresh
   coriander or mint
½ cup yoghurt
1 tablespoon ghee

Pilau:
1½ cups long grain rice
1 tablespoon ghee
1 onion, finely sliced
3 whole cloves
3 cardamom pods, bruised
1 small stick cinnamon
1 teaspoon taaza masala
   (page xxxii), optional
3 cups hot water
1½ teaspoons salt
¼ cup sultanas
½ cup green peas

Put lamb or beef and onion into a large bowl. Roast cummin seeds in a dry pan over medium heat, stirring constantly until they darken, then crush. Mix cummin, garlic, ginger, salt, garam masala and herbs into the yoghurt, then combine with lamb and onions in bowl and mix well. With wet hands form into small balls, no larger than marbles. Heat ghee in a frying pan and brown the meatballs on all sides, shaking pan rather than stirring, and taking care not to break them. Set aside.

Pilau: Wash rice if necessary and drain for at least 30 minutes. In a large saucepan heat ghee and fry the onion, cloves, cardamom pods and cinnamon stick until onions are golden. Stir in the green masala paste, then immediately add the rice and fry for 3 minutes, using a metal spoon. Add hot water, salt, sultanas and peas. Stir in meatballs. Bring to boil, cover tightly, then turn heat very low and cook for 20–25 minutes or until all liquid is absorbed. Serve hot.

Bisi Bellha Hoolli Annam
Rice with Lentils and Tamarind (Karnataka)   *Serves: 4–5*

½ cup toor dhal (page 62)
1 cup long grain rice
2¾ cups water
¼ teaspoon ground turmeric
1½ teaspoons salt
3 tablespoons oil
½ teaspoon asafoetida,
   optional
2 tablespoons coriander seeds
4 dried red chillies, stalks
   and seeds removed

small piece cinnamon stick
20 cloves
3 tablespoons freshly grated or
   desiccated coconut
500 g (1 lb) green beans
¼ cup tamarind pulp or
   2 teaspoons instant tamarind
1½ tablespoons mustard seed
12 curry leaves
2 tablespoons ghee
¼ cup raw cashews

A meal in one dish, combining rice, lentils and vegetables.

Wash the dhal and rice, drain well, then put into a saucepan with water, turmeric and salt, bring to the boil, cover and cook until water is absorbed, about 20 minutes.

Meanwhile heat 3 teaspoons oil and fry the asafoetida (if used) for about 3 minutes. Remove the asafoetida and fry the coriander and chillies for 3 or 4 minutes. Put asafoetida, coriander, chillies, cinnamon, cloves and coconut into electric blender, add just enough water to facilitate blending and blend until spices are finely ground.

Top and tail beans and cut into small pieces. Cook in lightly salted boiling water until almost tender. Drain, reserving liquid. Soak the tamarind pulp in ½ cup of this liquid, and squeeze to dissolve the pulp, then strain and discard seeds and fibres. If using instant tamarind, dissolve in the hot liquid, ground spice and coconut mixture and bring to the boil, cover and simmer 5 minutes. Add the cooked dhal and rice and stir well, taking care not to mash the grains. Heat the ghee in a small pan and fry the cashew nuts until golden. Pour the ghee over the rice and mix. Serve hot, garnished with the fried cashews.

Note: Slices of fried aubergine and potato are sometimes added to this dish.

Sultanpuri Pilau

Spiced Rice and Lamb (Uttar Pradesh)   *Serves: 4*

1½ cups long grain rice
750 g (1½ lb) lamb forequarter
 chops
4 cups water
1 small onion, chopped
2 cardamom pods, lightly
 bruised
2 bay leaves
small piece cinnamon stick
2½ teaspoons salt
½ cup milk
1 tablespoon ghee
2 tablespoons oil

1 large onion, finely sliced
1 tablespoon finely shredded
 fresh ginger
2 teaspoons finely sliced garlic
½ teaspoon black cummin seeds
2 fresh red chillies, seeded
 and sliced
⅛ teaspoon saffron strands or
 pinch powdered saffron
pinch red colouring powder

*This very simple yet delicious combination served as a main dish
needs only a fresh chutney, a raita (yoghurt cooler) and perhaps a
vegetable curry to make it a company meal.*

Wash rice well and leave to drain. Put lamb into a large saucepan
with water, the chopped onion, cardamom pods, bay leaves,
cinnamon stick and salt. Bring to the boil, then skim surface, cover
and simmer gently for at least 1 hour until meat is tender. Remove
meat from pan and leave until cool enough to handle. Measure
stock. If more than 2½ cups continue cooking with lid off pan until it
is reduced to this amount. Add milk to make 3 cups. Cut meat into
cubes, discarding bones and fat.

Heat ghee and oil in a large, heavy saucepan and fry the finely
sliced onion until soft. Add ginger and garlic and continue frying
and stirring frequently until they are golden. Remove to a plate. Add
meat to pan and fry, stirring, until meat is browned, remove with
slotted spoon and set aside with the fried onion mixture. Fry the
black cummin seeds and the chillies for 1 minute and set aside
separately. Put half the washed and drained rice into the saucepan
and spread with the meat and onion mixture, then cover with
remaining rice. Sprinkle the black cummin seeds and chillies over
rice. Reserve 1 tablespoon of milk and stock and gently pour the
stock over the rice. Bring to the boil, then turn heat very low, cover
tightly and allow to cook for 20 minutes.

Meanwhile, heat the reserved stock and dissolve the saffron in it. If saffron strands are used, pound them first in mortar and pestle. If powdered saffron is used, put it straight into the hot stock. Add a very little red colouring also to give a bright orange-red colour. When the rice has cooked for 20 minutes, pour the saffron liquid over the top. It will not colour many grains, but this is the way it should be. Replace the lid and leave for a further 5 minutes. Before serving, gently fork the coloured grains through the rice. Serve hot.

Thair Sadam

Rice with Yoghurt (South India)   *Serves: 4–6*

2½ cups long grain rice
4 cups water
2½ teaspoons salt
2 tablespoons ghee or oil
1 teaspoon black cummin seeds
1 teaspoon black mustard seeds

1 teaspoon urad dhal (page 62)
¼ teaspoon asafoetida, optional
3 fresh red or green chillies,
    seeded and sliced
3 cups yoghurt
salt to taste

In southern India, this dish is often served as the finale to a festive meal, but it may be presented as the meal itself, accompanied by curries and pickles.

Put well washed and drained rice into a saucepan with the water and salt. Bring quickly to the boil, then cover tightly, turn heat very low and cook for 20 minutes without lifting lid.

In another pan heat the ghee and fry the black cummin, mustard, dhal, asafoetida (if used) and chillies until the mustard seeds pop and the dhal is golden brown. Remove from heat, stir into the yoghurt and add a little salt to taste. Mix thoroughly with the cooked rice.

Masala Bhath

Spicy Rice Maharashtrian Style (Maharashtra)   *Serves: 6*

3 cups long grain rice
3 tablespoons ghee
3 tablespoons oil
3 large onions, finely sliced
5 cardamom pods, bruised
2 small sticks cinnamon
6 whole cloves
20 whole black peppercorns
½ teaspoon ground turmeric
5 cups hot water
3 teaspoons salt
½ cup raw cashew nuts,
    split in halves
2 sprigs fresh curry leaves or
    20 dried curry leaves
3 fresh green chillies, seeded
    and sliced
2 teaspoons black mustard
    seeds

Garnish:
2 tablespoons chopped fresh
    coriander
½ cup grated fresh coconut

Wash rice well and leave to drain in colander for at least 30 minutes.
In a large, heavy saucepan heat half the ghee and oil and fry the
onions and whole spices until onions are golden brown, stirring
frequently. Remove half the onions and set aside for garnish. Add
turmeric and rice to pan and fry, stirring with slotted metal spoon,
until all the grains are coated with the ghee. Add the hot water and
salt, stir well and bring to the boil. Cover with tightly fitting lid and
turn heat very low. Cook for 20–25 minutes without lifting lid.

Heat remaining ghee and oil in a small pan and fry the cashew
nuts until golden. Remove with slotted spoon. Fry the curry leaves,
green chillies and mustard seeds until the seeds pop. Pour over the
rice, lightly fork through. Dish up rice and garnish with the fried
cashews, chopped coriander leaves and grated fresh coconut.

Paratha
Flaky Wholemeal Bread   *Makes 12-14*

1½ cups atta flour
1½ cups plain flour or
   roti flour
1½ teaspoons salt

6-8 tablespoons ghee
1 cup water
extra ghee for cooking

Probably the favourite variety of Indian bread, parathas are rich, flaky and deliciously flavoured with ghee. Kebabs and parathas is a combination which is quite famous. A dear friend of my grandmother taught me her method of rolling and folding the parathas—the easiest and most successful one I've tried.

Sieve atta flour, plain flour and salt into a mixing bowl and rub in 1 tablespoon of the ghee. Add water, mix and knead dough as for chapatis (page 36). Cover dough with clear plastic and set aside for 1 hour.

Divide dough into 12-14 equal portions and roll each into a smooth ball. Melt ghee in a small saucepan over a low heat and cool slightly. Roll each ball of dough on a lightly floured board into a very thin circular shape. Pour 2 teaspoons of the melted ghee into the centre of each and spread lightly with the hand. With a knife make a cut from the centre of each circle to the outer edge. Starting at the cut edge, roll the dough closely into a cone shape. Pick it up, press the apex of the cone and the base towards each other and flatten slightly. You will now have a small, roughly circular lump of dough again. Lightly flour the board again and roll out the dough very gently, taking care not to press too hard and let the air out at the edges. The parathas should be as round as possible, but not as thinly rolled as the first time.

Cook on a hot griddle or heavy pan liberally greased with extra ghee, turning parathas and spreading with more ghee, until they are golden brown. Serve hot with grilled kebabs, sambals and podina chatni (page 139).

Note: The atta and plain or roti flour can be replaced by 3 cups of plain white flour.

Puris
Deep-fried Wholemeal Bread

Proceed as for chapatis (next recipe). When all the dough is rolled out heat approximately 2.5 cm (1 inch) of oil in a deep frying pan. When a faint haze rises from the oil, fry puris one at a time, over a moderate heat. Spoon hot oil continually over the cooking puri until it puffs and swells. Turn over and fry other side in the same way. When both sides are pale golden brown, drain on absorbent paper. Serve immediately with curries and bhajis.

Note: Puri is pronounced 'poo-ree'.

Chapatis
Unleavened Wholemeal Bread   *Makes 20–24*

3 cups atta or roti flour
1–1½ teaspoons salt, or
  to taste

1 tablespoon ghee or oil,
  optional
1 cup lukewarm water

Flat discs of unleavened bread, with a delightful flavour and chewy texture.

Put flour in mixing bowl, reserving about ½ cup for rolling out chapatis. Mix salt through the flour in the bowl, then rub in ghee or oil, if used. Add water all at once and mix to a firm but not stiff dough. Knead dough for at least 10 minutes (the more it is kneaded, the lighter the bread will be). Form dough into a ball, cover with clear plastic wrap and stand for 1 hour or longer. (If left overnight the chapatis will be very light and tender.)

Shape dough into balls about the size of a large walnut. Roll out each one on a lightly floured board (using reserved flour) to a circular shape as thin as a French crêpe. After rolling out chapatis, heat a griddle plate or heavy frying pan until very hot, and cook the chapatis, starting with those that were rolled first (the resting between rolling and cooking seems to make the chapatis lighter). Put chapati on griddle and leave for about 1 minute. Turn and cook other side another minute, pressing lightly around the edges of the chapati with a folded tea towel or an egg slice. This encourages bubbles to form and makes the chapatis light. As each one is cooked, wrap in a clean tea towel until all are ready. Serve immediately with butter, dry curries or vegetable dishes.

Note: In India, the chapatis are cooked on the tawa or griddle and are held for a moment or two right over the fire. This makes them puff up like balloons. You can do this over a gas flame, holding them with kitchen tongs.

Bhatura
Fried Wholemeal Bread (Punjab)   *Makes 12–14*

³⁄₄ cup yoghurt
2 teaspoons sugar
½ teaspoon bicarbonate of
   soda
1 cup plain flour

2½ cups atta flour
2 teaspoons salt
1 tablespoon ghee or butter
½ cup lukewarm water
oil for deep frying

A sort of sour-dough bread that is traditionally served with the preparation of chick peas called cholé (page 69).

Mix yoghurt, sugar, bicarbonate of soda and plain flour in a bowl, cover with muslin and leave overnight in a warm place to allow natural fermentation to take place. Sift the wholemeal flour and salt into a bowl, rub in the ghee or butter. Add the fermented mixture and the lukewarm water. Mix to a dough, adding as much extra plain flour as necessary. Knead hard for 10 minutes. Cover and leave in a warm place for about 2 or 3 hours. Divide into 12–14 portions.

Roll out each one thinly on a floured board to the size of a saucer. Fry one at a time in hot, deep oil, spooning oil on top. Bhaturas will puff and become golden when they are done. Remove with slotted spoon and drain on absorbent paper. Serve warm.

Besan Roti
Chick Pea Flour Bread (Uttar Pradesh)   *Makes about 15*

2 cups roti flour or atta flour
1 cup besan (chick pea flour)
2 teaspoons salt
½ teaspoon ground black
   pepper
1 tablespoon ghee or oil
2 fresh green chillies, seeded
   and finely chopped or
3 tablespoons finely chopped
   green pepper

3 tablespoons finely chopped
   coriander
3 tablespoons finely chopped
   spring onion
3 tablespoons finely chopped
   spinach
¼ teaspoon crushed ajowan
   seeds
1 cup water
ghee or oil for shallow frying

Sift both kinds of flour together with salt and pepper into a bowl.
Rub in ghee or oil and mix the other dry ingredients through. Add
water and mix to a dough, kneading firmly until it is smooth and
elastic. Cover with plastic wrap and set aside for 1 hour or longer.

Take balls of the dough and roll out on lightly floured board to the
size of a large saucer, and a thickness of about 2.5 mm (¹⁄₁₀ inch). Heat
a griddle or heavy frying pan and cook as for parathas (page 35).

Naan
Punjabi Leavened Bread   *Makes about 8 loaves*

30 g (1 oz) fresh compressed
   yeast or 1 sachet dried yeast
¾ cup lukewarm water
3 teaspoons sugar
½ cup yoghurt
1 egg, beaten

¼ cup melted ghee or butter
2 teaspoons salt
approximately 3½ cups plain
   flour
2 tablespoons poppy seeds or
   black cummin seeds

In a small warm bowl sprinkle yeast over ¼ cup warm water and
leave for a few minutes to soften, then stir to dissolve. Add 1

teaspoon of the sugar, stir, then leave in a warm place for 10 minutes or until it starts to froth. This is to test whether the yeast is live. If it does not froth start again with a fresh batch of yeast.

Stir yoghurt until smooth, then mix ¼ cup yoghurt with the rest of the sugar, the remaining ½ cup lukewarm water, egg, melted ghee or butter and salt. Stir in the yeast mixture. Put 2 cups flour into a bowl, make a well in the centre and pour in liquid mixture, beating well with a wooden spoon until it is a smooth batter. Add remaining flour a little at a time and when it gets too stiff to use the spoon, knead with the hands until a stiff dough is formed. Knead for 10–12 minutes or until dough is smooth and elastic, using as little extra flour as possible. Form dough into a ball, let it rest on board while preparing bowl. Heat bowl by running warm water into it and leaving for a few minutes. Dry bowl well, grease it, then put dough in bowl and turn it over so that the top is greased. Cover with a cloth and leave in a warm place until it doubles in size and a finger pushed into the dough leaves an impression. Punch down dough and divide into 8 balls, leave to rest 10 minutes.

Preheat oven to very hot 230°C (450°F). Put two ungreased baking trays into the oven to preheat.

Pat dough into circles keeping them thin in the centre and thicker around the rim then pull one end outwards, making a teardrop shape. They should be a handspan long and little more than half as wide at the base. Brush with remaining ¼ cup yoghurt and sprinkle with poppy or black cummin seeds.

Put 2 or 3 loaves on each baking tray. Bake about 10 minutes or until golden and puffed. If naan is not brown enough, put under a preheated grill for a minute or two. Serve warm or cool with tandoori murgh (page 92), Hussaini kebab (page 126) or mutton korma (page 116), and with dahi kachumbar (page 137) as an accompaniment.

Mithai Paratha
Sweet Flaky Wholemeal Bread   *Makes: 10*

1 cup toor or channa dhal
  (page 62)
1 cup sugar
2 tablespoons ghee
½ teaspoon ground cardamom
1½ cups atta flour

1½ cups roti or plain white
  flour
1 teaspoon salt
1 cup lukewarm water
extra ghee for cooking

These sweet parathas may be served as part of a meal, accompanied by savoury preparations and pickles. Children love them as a snack.

Wash the dhal and soak overnight. Next day cook in plenty of water until very tender. This takes some time and a pressure cooker may be used to good effect. Drain away any excess moisture and mash the dhal to a purée. For a very smooth result, push it through a sieve. Return the mashed dhal to a heavy saucepan, add sugar and 1 tablespoon ghee and cook over medium heat. The sugar will cause the mixture to become wet, but in about 10 minutes the mixture should thicken and become dry. Stir constantly, scraping mixture from side of pan. Remove from heat and turn mixture into a bowl, stir in cardamom and leave to cool.

Make a paratha dough by mixing both kinds of flour and the salt together, rubbing in the remaining ghee and adding water all at once. Knead 10 minutes until smooth and elastic. Set aside, covered, for at least 30 minutes. (If preferred, dough may be made with all white flour instead of wholemeal.) Divide dough into 10 portions. Take portions of dhal filling about the same size. Flatten the paratha dough to a small circle, place a ball of the filling on it and bring the dough together to completely enclose the filling, pressing edges together to seal. On a lightly floured surface roll out the parathas very gently, taking care not to break the dough and let the filling out. The parathas should be quite thin, and about the size of a large saucer.

Cook on a hot griddle or heavy pan, using a little ghee. Drizzle a little melted ghee over the top of the paratha and turn over to cook second side. Continue turning and cooking, adding more ghee as necessary, until paratha is golden on both sides.

Vegetables

India's vegetarian cuisine is unsurpassed in all the world. Small wonder, for this is an art that has developed over centuries. To be vegetarian in India is no deprivation. One does not miss eating meat, for the wonderful variety of vegetable preparations more than satisfies the gourmet.

Cooking vegetables the Indian way is learning to use every bit of goodness. Vegetables are never boiled and the water discarded. Rather they are braised, steamed, curried, fried, or simmered in a minimum of water and their own juices. Vegetables are cooked in a dry style called *bhaji*, puréed for *bartha* or spiced and made into fritters and a number of other dishes.

Vegetables should not be masked by too liberal uses of spices. Only a sprinkling of aromatic seeds or herbs is needed to give tantalising flavour. Sometimes they are cooked in coconut milk, giving richness and retaining their natural sweetness. There is something for everyone in India's vegetarian cuisine.

A visit to a market in Bangalore created a vivid impression. I had been to the huge markets in Delhi and Bombay and had been impressed by the array of fruits and vegetables there, but high on this plateau in Karnataka the variety was dazzling.

There were beans and gourds I recognised from years ago and many others I had never seen before. Piles of chillies of a dozen different kinds, baskets of tomatoes, fresh ginger, dried tamarind and turmeric roots, barrow loads of purple onions, bunches of glossy green curry leaves.

Many of the vegetables used in Indian cookery are becoming available in the west. But it isn't necessary to search for unusual vegetables. Commonplace potatoes, carrots, pumpkins, beans and peas are also popular in India and how different and delicious they are when cooked the Indian way.

The vegetables I have used in these recipes are readily obtainable – some for a short season and others the whole year round. I do urge that fresh vegetables are used, for frozen ones make a poor substitute.

Same ka Bhaji
Savoury Fried Beans (Karnataka)

Serves: 4–6

500 g (1 lb) green beans or
   snake beans
1 tablespoon oil or ghee
½ teaspoon black mustard seed
1 medium onion, finely·
   chopped
½ teaspoon finely grated
   fresh ginger
1 teaspoon ground turmeric

1 teaspoon garam masala
   (page xxx)
1 fresh red or green chilli,
   seeded and chopped
½ cup coconut milk (page xxxv)
1½ teaspoons salt or to taste

Top and tail beans, remove strings and cut them into 5 cm (2 inch) lengths. Heat the oil or ghee in a karahi or saucepan and fry the black mustard seeds until they pop. Add the onion and ginger and fry, stirring, until onion is soft and golden. Add turmeric, garam masala, chilli and the beans and fry for 2 or 3 minutes. Add coconut milk and salt and cook uncovered, stirring now and then, until beans are just tender.

Gobi Bhaji
Spicy Fried Cauliflower (Punjab)

Serves: 4

½ small cauliflower
1 green pepper
2 fresh red or green chillies
2 tablespoons oil
½ teaspoon black cummin
   seeds
½ teaspoon black mustard
   seeds

½ teaspoon cummin seeds
1 teaspoon taaza masala
   (page xxxii) or ½ teaspoon
   grated fresh ginger and
   ½ teaspoon crushed garlic
1 teaspoon salt
1 tablespoon water

Break cauliflower into florets, seed the pepper and cut into strips, seed and slice the chillies.

   Heat oil in saucepan and fry the seeds, stirring, until the mustard seeds pop. Add the green masala paste, salt, and the vegetables and stir and toss to mix thoroughly with the spice mixture.

Add water and immediately put the lid on the pan to trap the steam. Cook covered over medium heat, shaking pan occasionally, for about 8 minutes or until cauliflower is tender but still crisp. Serve with rice or chapatis.

Karela Baigan Bhaji
Fried Bittergourd and Aubergine (Punjab)   *Serves: 4–6*

1 large or 2 small bittergourds	2 teaspoons finely grated fresh ginger
1 medium or 2 small aubergines	½ teaspoon ground turmeric
3 medium onions	approximately ¼ cup hot water
2 fresh red or green chillies	1 teaspoon salt
4 tablespoons oil	
½ teaspoon panch phora (page xxxi)	

Fresh bittergourds or karela as they are called in India are sold in Chinese greengrocers as 'bittermelon'. Buy these whenever possible but if canned ones are used add them only during the last few minutes of cooking.

Halve the bittergourds lengthways and if seeds are large and mature remove and discard them. If the bittergourds are tender, the seeds may be left in. Slice thickly lengthways, then cut into 5 cm (2 inch) lengths. Wash but do not peel aubergines and cut into small cubes. Chop the onions and seed and slice the chillies.

Heat oil in a heavy saucepan and add the panch phora. Fry for 1 minute, then add onions and chillies. Fry, stirring occasionally until onions are golden. Add ginger and turmeric, then fry the bittergourd for 3 minutes, stirring. Add aubergine and salt. Stir well, adding about ¼ cup hot water or just enough to cover base of pan. Cover and cook on low heat for 20 minutes or until the vegetables are cooked through. Stir occasionally, being careful not to mash the pieces of bittergourd and aubergine. When vegetables are tender, if there is much liquid left in pan cook uncovered so that most of the liquid evaporates. Serve with rice or chapatis.

Bhari Simla Mirich
Stuffed Chillies (Punjab)

Serves: 4

8 large, mild chillies
   (or 4 peppers)
1 large onion, roughly chopped
1 ripe tomato, peeled and
   roughly chopped
1 teaspoon chopped fresh
   ginger
2 fresh red chillies, seeded
4 tablespoons oil
½ cup hot water
½ teaspoon garam masala
   (page xxx)

Potato Filling:
500 g (1 lb) potatoes
2 tablespoons oil
½ teaspoon ground turmeric
1 medium onion, finely
   chopped
2 fresh green chillies, seeded
   and finely chopped
¾ teaspoon salt
¼ teaspoon ground black
   pepper

Garnish:
2 tablespoons chopped fresh
   coriander, optional

Use large, long, mild chillies for this rather than peppers.

Wash mild chillies and dry them. Cut off a slice from the top and with pointed knife remove seeds and pith from the centre. Stuff with potato filling, using the handle of a teaspoon to fill them right to the end.

Put onion, tomato, ginger and red chillies into electric blender and blend to a purée. Heat the oil in a frying pan or saucepan and fry the filled chillies, turning them gently, until almost cooked. Remove chillies to a plate and add the blended mixture to the oil left in the pan. Stir and fry until the mixture smells cooked and oil separates from the mass. Add hot water, cover and cook over low heat for a few more minutes. Stir well, taking care it does not stick to the pan. Lay the chillies in the mixture, sprinkle with garam masala, cover and cook for a further 5 minutes. Sprinkle with chopped fresh coriander, if used, and serve with rice or chapatis.

Potato Filling: Peel and dice the potatoes and cook in lightly salted boiling water until soft. Drain well. Heat the oil in a small pan and add the turmeric. Add onion and chillies and fry, stirring now and then, until soft. Remove from heat, add to the potatoes together with salt and pepper and mix thoroughly. While potatoes should not be mashed, they should be sufficiently soft to hold together.

Baigan Bartha
Aubergine Purée (Punjab)   *Serves: 6*

2 medium aubergines
2 tablespoons oil
2 medium onions, chopped
1 teaspoon ground coriander
1 teaspoon ground cummin
½ teaspoon chilli powder,
  optional
1 large ripe tomato, chopped

3 tablespoons finely chopped
  fresh coriander
3 spring onions, finely chopped
1 teaspoon salt or to taste
½ teaspoon garam masala
  (page xxx)

Aubergines cooked to a spicy purée are popular throughout India, but perhaps nowhere more so than in the Punjab. In this recipe the aubergines are roasted first, which adds a certain smoky flavour.

Roast aubergines over gas flame, or hot coals, or under grill, until the skin is thoroughly blackened all over and the aubergine itself is soft to the touch. When cool enough to handle, remove all skin under running cold water. Mash or chop roughly.

In a heavy saucepan heat oil and fry the onion until lightly browned. Add ground spices and stir for a few seconds, then add tomato, aubergines, fresh coriander, spring onions and salt. Cover and cook on low heat until liquid evaporates and it becomes a purée thick enough to scoop up with pieces of chapati. Add garam masala and simmer, uncovered, for a few minutes longer. Serve hot or cold as an accompaniment to chapatis, parathas or rice.

Tamatar Alu Bhaji Tarkari
Aubergine and Potato Curry (Bengal)   *Serves: 6*

2 small aubergines
2 large potatoes
2 large ripe tomatoes
1 large onion
2 fresh green chillies
1 bunch spinach
3 tablespoons mustard oil

1½ teaspoons finely chopped
   ginger
½ teaspoon cummin seeds,
   crushed
½ teaspoon ground turmeric
1 teaspoon salt
1 teaspoon jaggery or brown
   sugar

Wash aubergines and cut in small cubes. Peel and dice the potatoes, peel and chop the tomatoes. Finely chop the onion. Seed and slice the chillies. Wash the spinach in several changes of water, remove tough stalks and roughly chop the leaves.

Heat oil in a deep frying pan or karahi and let it get smoking hot. Fry the potatoes until golden, remove from pan. Fry the aubergine and remove from pan. Add the onion and fry until soft and golden, add ginger, cummin and turmeric and fry for 1 minute. Add chillies, tomatoes and salt, then add the potatoes, aubergine and spinach. Stir. Cover and cook on low heat until spinach is soft, adding ½ cup water if necessary. Add jaggery or sugar, stir and cook uncovered until liquid evaporates. Serve with rice or chapatis.

Dum Gobi
Spiced Steamed Cauliflower (Uttar Pradesh)   *Serves: 4*

1 small cauliflower
2 tablespoons butter or ghee
salt and pepper to taste
¼ cup finely chopped cashews

2 teaspoons chironji nuts or
   sunflower seeds
½ teaspoon garam masala
   (page xxx)

Steam the cauliflower until half cooked. Put into an oven dish, spread with half the butter or ghee and season with salt and pepper.

Cover and bake in a moderate oven, 180°C (350°F), until tender, then remove lid and brown under the grill. In remaining butter or ghee lightly fry the cashews until golden, add chironji or sunflower seeds and fry a little longer. Mix in the spice and sprinkle over the cauliflower. Serve hot.

Lasan Kari

Garlic Curry (Tamil Nadu)   *Serves: 4*

250 g (8 oz) garlic
8–10 small onions, preferably red onions
8 large fresh mild chillies
2 tablespoons coconut oil (or other vegetable oil)
1 teaspoon fenugreek seeds
1 teaspoon chilli powder

½ teaspoon ground turmeric
1½ cups coconut milk (page xxxv)
½ teaspoon salt, or to taste
2 teaspoons tamarind pulp or ½ teaspoon instant tamarind
¼ cup hot water

In this unusual curry, cloves of garlic are treated as a vegetable. If 250 g (8 oz) garlic sounds terrifying to you, tone down the content by substituting small new potatoes, halved or quartered, for some of the garlic.

Choose garlic with as large individual cloves as you can find. Peel the cloves but leave them whole. Peel the onions. Cut stalks from the chillies but leave them intact, with the seeds inside.

Heat oil in a heavy saucepan and fry the garlic, onions and chillies over gentle heat, not letting them brown too much. Remove from pan. Add fenugreek seeds to the oil in pan and stir over low heat just until they are golden. Add the chilli powder and turmeric, fry for a few seconds, then add the coconut milk, salt and stir while bringing slowly to simmering point. Return the garlic, onions and chillies and allow to simmer, uncovered, until garlic cloves are soft, about 30 minutes depending on size. Meanwhile dissolve tamarind in hot water, strain into curry for last 10 minutes of cooking. Serve with hot white rice.

Bhendi Pakorha
Okra Fried in Batter (Punjab)   *Serves: 4*

250 g (8 oz) small, tender okra
1 teaspoon oil
2 teaspoons ground coriander
2 teaspoons ground rice
¼ teaspoon ground turmeric
1 teaspoon finely grated fresh
  ginger
2 fresh green chillies, seeded
  and finely chopped
1 teaspoon salt
squeeze of lemon juice to taste

Batter:
½ cup besan (chick pea flour)
½ cup self-raising flour
approximately ¾ cup water
½ teaspoon garam masala
  (page xxx)
½ teaspoon chilli powder
1 teaspoon crushed garlic
1 teaspoon salt
oil for deep frying

Wash okra, wipe dry with kitchen paper and make a slit on one side
of each pod. Heat the oil and fry the coriander, ground rice,
turmeric, ginger and chillies, stirring constantly, until the spices are
golden brown. Remove from heat, mix in the salt and a squeeze of
lemon juice to taste. Put a little of this mixture in the slit made in
each okra pod.

Mix the besan and self-raising flours smoothly with the water to
make a fairly liquid dipping batter. Stir in the garam masala, chilli
powder, garlic and salt. Heat enough oil to deep fry the okra. Dip
each one into the batter and drop into the hot oil. Fry over medium-
high heat until golden brown. Drain on absorbent paper and serve
as an accompaniment to rice and curries.

Bhendi Bhaji
Fried Okra (Uttar Pradesh)   *Serves: 4*

500 g (1 lb) okra
2 tablespoons ghee or oil
½ teaspoon panch phora
  (page xxxi)
1 large onion, finely chopped
1 teaspoon ground coriander
½ teaspoon ground turmeric

½ teaspoon chilli powder
½ teaspoon salt, or to taste
1 teaspoon amchur (dried green
  mango) or 1 tablespoon lemon
  juice
½ teaspoon garam masala
  (page xxx)

Okra (bhendi) is a type of bean that has been known in Asia for a long time. It originated in Africa whence it made its way to America and is widely used in Creole cookery. Recognise okra by the slightly furry, striated pods shaped like a furled umbrella. To test for tenderness, bend the thin tip of the bean – if fresh and tender it will snap clean off, if old and tough it will bend.

Wash the okra, cut off and discard stem ends and slice into bite-size pieces.

Heat ghee or oil and fry the panch phora for a minute. Add onion and fry, stirring, until onion is soft. Add coriander, turmeric, chilli and salt. Add okra, stir, cover and cook on low heat, stirring now and then, until okra is tender. Sprinkle with the amchur or lemon juice and the garam masala. Toss to mix and serve with rice or chapatis.

Sukhe Alu
Dry Potato Curry (Punjab)   *Serves: 4–6*

500 g (1 lb) potatoes
1½ tablespoons ghee or oil
1 teaspoon panch phora
(page xxxi)
1 medium onion, finely
chopped
2 tablespoons chopped fresh
mint or coriander

1 teaspoon ground turmeric
1½ teaspoons salt
½ teaspoon chilli powder,
optional
¼ cup hot water
1 teaspoon garam masala
(page xxx)
1 tablespoon lemon juice

Peel potatoes, cut into quarters or, if very large, into cubes. In a heavy saucepan with lid, heat ghee or oil and add the panch phora. When mustard seeds in the panch phora begin to pop add the onion and fry, stirring, until soft. Add chopped herbs, turmeric, salt and chilli powder (if used). Add potatoes, stir well, sprinkle with hot water and cover pan tightly. Cook over very low heat for 20 minutes, shaking pan occasionally to prevent potatoes sticking. Sprinkle with garam masala and lemon juice, replace lid and cook for a further 10 minutes or until potatoes are tender. Serve with chapatis, parathas or rice.

Alu Mattar Rasa
Potato and Pea Curry (Uttar Pradesh)   *Serves: 6*

1 large onion
1 fresh red chilli
2 teaspoons chopped fresh
  ginger
2 tablespoons oil
½ teaspoon ground turmeric
2 teaspoons ground coriander
1 cup shelled peas
1 cup hot water
1 teaspoon salt
500 g (1 lb) potatoes, peeled
  and cubed
2 large ripe tomatoes, peeled
  and chopped
3 tablespoons yoghurt
1 teaspoon garam masala
  (page xxx)

Garnish:
2 tablespoons chopped fresh
  coriander

Peel and roughly chop the onion. Seed the chilli, discard stalk, put onion, chilli and ginger into electric blender and blend to a purée, adding a little water if necessary to facilitate blending. Heat the oil in a heavy saucepan and fry the blended mixture, stirring, for 3 or 4 minutes. Add turmeric and coriander and fry a little longer. Add peas, hot water and salt, cover and cook for 10 minutes before adding the potatoes. If the peas are very young and tender they may be put in together with the potatoes. When peas and potatoes are half cooked, add tomatoes and continue cooking for a few minutes longer, then mix in the yoghurt stirred until smooth with a little water. Simmer until liquid is thick. Sprinkle with garam masala and stir gently to mix. Serve garnished with fresh coriander.

Alu Dum
Steamed Potatoes (Kashmir)   *Serves: 4*

500 g (1 lb) small new potatoes
1 small onion, roughly chopped
1 teaspoon chopped garlic
1 teaspoon chopped fresh
  ginger
1 tablespoon lemon juice
1 tablespoon water
1 teaspoon salt
1 tablespoon ghee or oil
1 small cinnamon stick
3 cardamom pods, bruised
2 whole cloves
1 bay leaf, crumbled
½ teaspoon ground turmeric

Garnish:
½ teaspoon cummin seed
½ cup yoghurt
½ teaspoon garam masala
  (page xxx)
2 tablespoons chopped fresh
  coriander or 2 fresh chillies,
  seeded and sliced

Scrub potatoes, do not peel. Put into a saucepan with just enough water to almost cover, bring to the boil and boil for 5 minutes with lid on pan. Drain immediately and with a fine skewer prick the potatoes lightly all over.

Put onion, garlic, ginger, lemon juice, 1 tablespoon water and salt in electric blender and blend to a purée. If blender is not available chop onion finely, crush garlic and finely grate the peeled ginger. Heat ghee or oil in saucepan and fry the cinnamon, cardamom, cloves and bay leaf for 2 minutes. Add the turmeric and stir, then add the blended mixture and fry, stirring, until the mixture smells cooked. Rinse out blender container with about 2 tablespoons extra water, add to pan with the potatoes and stir well. Cover pan tightly, turn heat very low and allow to steam for 15 minutes or until potatoes are cooked.

Roast cummin seeds in a dry pan, stirring constantly until dark brown. Combine yoghurt with garam masala, roasted cummin seeds roughly crushed or pounded, and a pinch of salt. Serve potatoes with yoghurt mixture spooned over and sprinkled with fresh coriander or, if preferred, fresh chillies.

Alu Mattar Bhaji

Savoury Potatoes and Peas (Uttar Pradesh)   *Serves: 4*

500 g (1 lb) potatoes
250 g (8 oz) fresh green peas
  or 1 cup frozen peas
2 tablespoons ghee or oil
2 medium onions, finely
  chopped
1 teaspoon finely grated fresh
  ginger

1 teaspoon black mustard seeds
½ teaspoon black cummin
  seeds
½ teaspoon ground turmeric
½ teaspoon chilli powder
1½ teaspoons salt
¾ cup hot water

Peel and dice potatoes, shell peas. Heat ghee or oil in a heavy saucepan and fry the onions and ginger, mustard and cummin seeds. When onions are soft and golden add the ground turmeric, chilli powder and salt. Toss potatoes and peas in this mixture for 5 minutes, then add hot water, cover tightly and cook on low heat for 30 minutes.

Sagu

Spiced Yellow Pumpkin (Karnataka)   *Serves: 4*

500 g (1 lb) yellow pumpkin
2 tablespoons oil
3 tablespoons toor dhal
  (page 62)
1 teaspoon black mustard seeds
10 curry leaves
1 teaspoon finely chopped
  garlic

2 teaspoons ground coriander
1 teaspoon ground cummin
½ teaspoon ground turmeric
1 teaspoon salt or to taste
3 tablespoons fresh grated
  coconut or desiccated
  coconut

Peel and seed the pumpkin and cut into cubes. Heat the oil in a saucepan and gently fry the dhal, mustard seeds and curry leaves until dhal is golden and mustard seeds pop. Add the garlic, fry for a minute longer, then add the ground spices and stir well. Put in the pumpkin and just enough water to almost cover the vegetable. Add salt. Cover and simmer until pumpkin is half cooked, then sprinkle in the coconut and continue cooking until pumpkin is soft.

Palak Panir
Spinach with Fresh Cheese (Punjab)   *Serves: 4–5*

250 g (8 oz) fresh spinach leaves
(without stems) or other
greens
1 tablespoon dried fenugreek
leaves, optional
250 g (8 oz) panir (page xxiii)
or ricotta
oil for deep frying
1 tablespoon ghee
½ teaspoon ground turmeric

1½ cups hot water
¼ teaspoon black cummin
seeds
small pinch asafoetida, optional
1 tablespoon ground coriander
½ teaspoon chilli powder
½ teaspoon finely grated fresh
ginger
1 teaspoon salt
½ teaspoon sugar
1 cup yoghurt

Indian housewives make fresh cheese, panir, as described on page xxiii. But it is simpler to use ready-made ricotta cheese.

Put the well-washed spinach leaves into a pan with the water that clings to them, add the fenugreek leaves (if used), cover and steam until spinach is soft. Drain well and chop finely.

Cut the ricotta into cubes and spread on absorbent paper for a few minutes so that surface moisture is absorbed. In a small, deep frying pan or karahi heat enough oil in which to deep fry the cubes of ricotta. Add a tablespoon of ghee to flavour the oil. When oil is very hot, fry a handful of ricotta cubes at a time. Have ready the turmeric stirred into 1 cup of hot water and when the ricotta is pale golden lift out on a slotted spoon and drop the cubes into the turmeric water. Repeat until all the ricotta is fried, leave in the water for about 5 minutes, then drain.

Heat about 2 tablespoons of the oil in a saucepan and add the black cummin seeds, asafoetida, coriander, chilli powder and ginger. Stir and fry briefly, taking care not to burn the spices. Add the spinach and salt and stir for a minute or two, then add about ½ cup hot water and the sugar. Simmer for 5 minutes. Stir the yoghurt until it is smooth, add it to the spinach and stir well. Add cubes of panir and simmer for 10 minutes longer. Serve hot with rice or chapatis.

Palak Sabzi ki Bhaji
Spinach with Mixed Vegetables (Maharashtra)   *Serves: 4–6*

1 bunch spinach
500 g (1 lb) pumpkin
250 g (8 oz) okra or french
  beans
½ cup fresh peas
2 tablespoons oil
1 teaspoon black mustard seeds

1 medium onion, finely
  chopped
1 teaspoon finely grated fresh
  ginger
½ teaspoon ground turmeric
1 cup hot water
½ cup raw cashews

Wash the spinach well, discard any tough stems and roughly chop
the leaves. Cut pumpkin into small cubes. String beans, if used, and
cut into short lengths.

Heat the oil in a karahi or saucepan and fry the mustard seeds
until they begin to pop. Add the onion and ginger and fry, stirring
now and then, until onion is soft. Add turmeric and fry for 1 minute
longer.

Add hot water, cashews and all the vegetables, cover and simmer
until they are tender, then remove lid and cook, stirring frequently,
until liquid is reduced. Serve with rice or chapatis. If serving with
rice, leave rather more liquid; if serving with chapatis, allow it to
reach a drier consistency.

Palak Alu
Spinach with Potatoes (Maharashtra Parsi)   *Serves: 4*

500 g (1 lb) new potatoes
1 bunch spinach
2 tablespoons ghee or oil
1 teaspoon black mustard
  seeds
1 teaspoon cummin seeds
½ teaspoon ground turmeric

½ teaspoon ground coriander
½ teaspoon ground cummin
2 fresh green chillies, slit and
  seeds removed
1 teaspoon salt or to taste
approximately ½ cup water
½ teaspoon grated nutmeg

Scrub the potatoes well and cut into small cubes. Wash the spinach
in several changes of water. Discard tough stems and put into a large
saucepan with just the water that clings to the leaves. Cover and

steam for 10 minutes or until tender, then chop roughly. Do not discard any liquid in pan.

In a large frying pan or karahi heat the ghee or oil and fry mustard and cummin seeds until mustard seeds pop. Cover pan or they will fly all over the stove. Add turmeric, coriander, cummin and the chillies. Add potatoes, stir and fry for a few minutes, then add salt and about ½ cup water, cover and cook for 10 minutes. Add spinach, stir, cover and cook for 5 or 10 minutes longer. Sprinkle nutmeg over and serve with rice or chapatis.

Cho Chori
Spicy Dried Vegetables (Bengal)   *Serves: 4*

3 medium carrots
2 medium potatoes
12 tender green beans
2 firm ripe tomatoes
2 tablespoons mustard oil or
   other vegetable oil
2 teaspoons black mustard
   seeds
2 dried red chillies, optional
2 onions, finely chopped
1 teaspoon finely chopped garlic

1 teaspoon finely chopped
   fresh ginger
1 teaspoon ground coriander
1 teaspoon ground cummin
½ teaspoon chilli powder,
   optional
1 teaspoon salt
2–3 tablespoons water
½ teaspoon garam masala,
   optional (page xxx)

Peel and dice the carrots and potatoes. Top and tail the beans and cut them into short lengths, the same size as the diced vegetables. Peel and dice the tomatoes.

Heat oil in a saucepan or karahi and fry the mustard seeds and chillies until the seeds pop. Add onions, garlic and ginger and fry, stirring, until golden. Add coriander, cummin and chilli powder (if used) and fry for a few seconds, then add vegetables and salt and toss until coated with the spices and oil. Add water, cover and cook 15 minutes or until vegetables are tender, stirring gently every 5 minutes and adding a little extra water if necessary. Sprinkle with garam masala, if used, towards end of cooking. Serve with rice or chapatis.

ᴀ́rbi ki Kari

Yam Curry (Gujarat)   *Serves: 3–4*

500 g (1 lb) yam or sweet potato
oil for deep frying
1 tablespoon ghee
2 medium onions, finely
  chopped
2 teaspoons finely grated ginger
2 fresh red or green chillies,
  seeded and chopped
1 teaspoon ground coriander
1 teaspoon ground cummin

½ teaspoon ground turmeric
½ teaspoon chilli powder,
  optional
½ teaspoon garam masala
  (page xxx)
1 teaspoon salt
1 tablespoon chopped fresh
  coriander
lemon juice, optional

Wash, peel and dice the yam or sweet potato and soak in lightly
salted water for 30 minutes. Drain well, and dry on absorbent paper.
Heat enough oil for deep frying and add ghee to give it flavour. Fry
the yam, not crowding the pan too much, until the pieces are golden
brown. Lift from oil on slotted spoon and drain on paper.

When all the yam has been fried, pour off the oil, leaving about 2
tablespoons. Fry the onion, ginger and chillies over medium heat,
stirring frequently, until onion is soft and golden. Add all the ground
spices and fry for another minute, stirring. Add the yam, sprinkle
with salt and fresh coriander and toss over low heat for 5 minutes. If
liked, add a squeeze of lemon juice. Serve hot.

ᴀ́viyal

Mixed Vegetables with Coconut (Kerala)   *Serves: 6–8*

About 6 cups mixed vegetables
  cut into julienne strips—
  carrots, french beans,
  courgettes, pumpkin,
  peppers, aubergines, chayote,
  cucumber, etc.
½ cup fresh green peas
½ cup freshly grated coconut
  or 3 tablespoons desiccated
  coconut

1 cup water
1 teaspoon cummin seeds
1 teaspoon chopped garlic
2 fresh green chillies, seeded
½ cup thick coconut milk
  (page xxx)
1½ teaspoons salt
6 curry leaves
2 teaspoons coconut oil

This is one of the most popular ways of serving vegetables in South India. The predominant flavouring is from coconut, for coconut palms grow in abundance along the coastline. To be truly authentic, a small spoonful of coconut oil should be stirred into this dish at the end, but even without this, it is a fine dish and one that gives vegetables a starring role.

In a saucepan bring to the boil enough lightly salted water to cover one kind of vegetable. Boil each vegetable separately, just long enough to make it tender but not soft and mushy. Take out vegetables on slotted spoon and put them in a bowl. Use the same water for all the vegetables, adding a little water at a time as it boils away, but keeping the quantity small. Save the cooking liquid.

In a blender put the coconut, water, cummin seeds, garlic and chillies. Blend on high speed until the coconut is very finely ground. Put this into the saucepan with the vegetable stock, add the coconut milk, salt and curry leaves and bring to the boil. Add the vegetables, simmer uncovered for 5 minutes. Stir in coconut oil and serve hot with rice.

Tamatar Bartha
Tomato Purée (Punjab)   *Serves: 4*

4 large ripe tomatoes
2 tablespoons ghee or oil
1 small onion, finely chopped
1 teaspoon finely chopped
   fresh ginger
1 fresh green chilli, seeded
   and chopped

2 tablespoons chopped fresh
   coriander
½ teaspoon ground black
   pepper
½ teaspoon salt or to taste

Grill whole tomatoes over gas flame or under electric grill until skins wrinkle. Peel and chop. Heat ghee or oil in a saucepan or karahi and fry the onion and ginger until golden. Add tomatoes and remaining ingredients. Cover and cook until the tomatoes are a thick pulp and most of the liquid evaporates. Serve with rice or chapatis.

Alu Bhaji

Spicy Fried Potatoes   *Serves: 4*

500 g (1 lb) potatoes
3 tablespoons oil
1 teaspoon black mustard seeds
½ teaspoon ground turmeric
1 large onion, finely sliced

1 or 2 fresh green chillies,
   seeded and sliced
1½ teaspoons salt
¼ cup hot water
1 tablespoon lemon juice

Boil potatoes in their skins until just tender. Peel and dice. Heat the
oil in a saucepan and fry the mustard seeds until they pop. Add the
turmeric, sliced onions and chillies and fry until onions are soft and
golden. Add the salt and water, bring to the boil, add potatoes, cover
and cook until liquid is absorbed. Remove from heat. Sprinkle with
lemon juice and stir well.

Saag

Greens Cooked Kashmiri Style (Kashmir)   *Serves: 4*

500 g (1 lb) washed and cleaned
   green leaves
2 tablespoons mustard oil
⅛ teaspoon powdered
   asafoetida, optional
½ teaspoon cummin seeds
1 teaspoon dried fenugreek
   leaves, optional

1 teaspoon grated fresh ginger
½ teaspoon ground turmeric
½ teaspoon ground fennel
2 fresh green chillies, seeded
   and sliced
1 cup diced potato, optional
1 teaspoon salt or to taste

*Use spinach, radish or broccoli leaves or any other leafy greens for
this recipe. Some leaves give out a lot of moisture and will not need
any water added, but those that require longer cooking may need a
small amount of water.*

Put the washed greens in a colander to drain. Heat oil in a karahi or
saucepan and add asafoetida, cummin seeds, fenugreek leaves and
ginger. Fry for 1 minute, stirring. Add the remaining ingredients,
including the greens, stir well. Cover and cook until potato is soft,
about 10 minutes. Add a little water if necessary. Serve with rice.

Sabzi Bhaji

Mixed Vegetables, Sindhi Style   *Serves: 4*

2 large carrots
2 large potatoes
2 medium onions
2 fresh red or green chillies
1 tablespoon ground coriander
1½ teaspoons ground turmeric
2 tablespoons ghee
2 tablespoons oil

1½ teaspoons finely grated
    fresh ginger
½ cup chopped fresh coriander
2 firm ripe tomatoes, peeled
    and diced
1 cup yoghurt
1½ teaspoons salt
lemon wedges or lemon juice
    to taste

Peel carrots and potatoes and cut both in julienne strips. Finely chop the onions and seed and finely slice the chillies. Combine all in a bowl, sprinkle the coriander and turmeric over and toss well. Leave for half an hour.

In a large saucepan heat the ghee and oil and fry the ginger, stirring, until golden. Add the mixed vegetables and fry for a few minutes. Stir in half the fresh coriander, tomatoes, yoghurt, and salt. Cover and cook for 10–15 minutes or until vegetables are tender. Serve hot with the remaining fresh coriander sprinkled over and accompanied by wedges of lemon or, if preferred, add lemon juice to taste. Serve with plain rice or bhuna kitchri (page 24), chapatis or puris.

Soups, Lentils and Milk Curd Dishes

Lentils, cheese and curds (yoghurt) are very important in Indian diets, especially for vegetarians as they supply the necessary protein. Hardly a meal is served that does not include lentils in some form. There are many varieties of dried beans and lentils. Dried beans are, for the most part, made into thick, dry curries for eating with Indian bread and the split, hulled lentils are used for the wet dishes which can best be described as soups, though they are not served as a first course. They are put on the table along with rice, curries, chutneys and other accompaniments and are sipped during the meal or poured over rice to moisten it.

There are whole lentils and those which have been husked and split, and these are called *dhal*. Thus you can have whole *moong* *(moong saboot)* or split and husked *moong (moong dhal)*, whole black gram *(urad dhal)*, and so on. I have listed the more commonly used lentils on the next page. All these are available in good Asian food shops and most of them in health food stores. The other two main sources of protein in diets that are either purely vegetarian or that feature meat very seldom are fresh cheese and yoghurt.

Fresh home-made cheese is used as a main ingredient in many dishes such as *chaman* and *palak panir*, and yoghurt appears at practically every meal. If it is not in some preparation it is served plain in a little bowl, to be eaten with or after the rest of the meal.

Western society has recently recognised the health-giving properties of yoghurt and it has become something of a fad, appearing in many flavours and as a frozen dessert but in countries where yoghurt is an important part of the daily diet it is always served plain and unflavoured. In many Indian households a batch of yoghurt is made every day, using a spoonful from the previous day's yoghurt. And if it is not made at home, it is easy enough to buy.

Making yoghurt in a yoghurt maker is foolproof, but it is also easily made in a wide-mouthed vacuum flask. Simply warm the flask with hot water, stir 1 tablespoon of yoghurt into 3 cups of lukewarm milk, pour into the warmed flask, cover and leave for 4 hours. When it is set remove the cover and store the yoghurt in the refrigerator.

Fresh cheese is easy to make at home (see page xxii). An alternative is to buy fresh ricotta cheese and cut it into cubes or slices. Treat it more gently than you would panir, however, because it is softer and more crumbly. There is also a type of fresh pecorino that does not melt when heated and this may be used instead of panir.

DHAL OR LENTILS: Lentils are of major importance in the Indian diet, as they are the chief source of protein, especially among the countless vegetarians. Lentils are the seeds of leguminous plants. Dhal means a seed that has been split in half and had the skin removed.

1 **Mattar ki dhal**—split peas, both yellow and green.
2 **Lobia**—black-eyed beans, whole.
3 **Channa dhal**—Bengal gram, skin removed.
4 **Masoor dhal**—red lentils, split and skin removed.
5 **Kabuli channa**—chick peas, whole.
6 **Rajma**—red kidney beans. The same name is sometimes applied to the variegated bean known as *borlotti*.
7 **Malka masoor**—the whole lentil sold as green lentils or brown lentils has a greeny-brown seed coat. Soak before cooking.
8 **Toor dhal**—(also known as *arhar dhal*). Red gram dhal.
9 **Moong saboot**—green gram, whole. The common name is mung bean and it is a very small bean with a moss green coat.
10 **Moong dhal**—green gram split, husked. Once the green coat is removed the inside is a pale yellow.
11 **Urad dhal**—black gram split, husked. The whole black gram, which is about the size of green gram, is used mostly in the cooking of the Punjab, but very infrequently in its whole form. When divested of its black seed coat it is a greyish white colour and when soaked, ground and set aside for a few hours, it has the property of fermenting and making the mixtures in which it is used very light and spongy.

Rasam

Pepper Water (South India)   *Serves: 6*

1 tablespoon tamarind pulp or
  1 teaspoon instant tamarind
1 cup hot water
1 teaspoon sliced garlic
½ teaspoon ground black
  pepper
1 teaspoon ground cummin

4 cups cold water
2 teaspoons salt
2 tablespoons chopped fresh
  coriander
2 teaspoons oil
1 teaspoon black mustard seeds
8 curry leaves

These thin soups are served as a digestive, either to be spooned over rice or taken at the end of a meal.

Soak tamarind pulp in hot water for 10 minutes, then squeeze to dissolve pulp in the water. Strain, discarding seeds and fibres. Alternatively dissolve instant tamarind in hot water. Put tamarind liquid, garlic, pepper, cummin, cold water, salt and coriander into a saucepan and bring to the boil. Turn heat down immediately and simmer for 10 minutes. In a small saucepan heat the oil and fry mustard seeds and curry leaves until leaves are brown. Add to the simmering soup and serve.

Sambar

Lentil and Vegetable Soup (South India)   *Serves: 6*

1 cup split peas (mattar ki dhal), red lentils (masoor dhal) or toor dhal
6 cups water
1 tablespoon tamarind pulp or 1 teaspoon instant tamarind
1 cup hot water
2 tablespoons oil
1 tablespoon ground coriander
2 teaspoons ground cummin
½ teaspoon ground black pepper
½ teaspoon chilli powder
½ teaspoon ground turmeric
⅛ teaspoon asafoetida
3 cups mixed vegetables (aubergines, marrow, beans, pumpkin, cubed)
2 fresh green chillies, seeded and sliced
2½ teaspoons salt
½ teaspoon black mustard seeds
1 small onion, finely sliced

Wash the dhal well and soak overnight, or for 2 hours. Drain and put in a saucepan with the water and simmer until soft. Soak tamarind pulp in hot water and squeeze to dissolve the pulp. Strain, discarding seeds and fibres. Alternatively dissolve instant tamarind in hot water. Add tamarind liquid to lentils.

In another pan heat 1 tablespoon oil and fry the ground spices and asafoetida on low heat, stirring, for a minute or two. Pour the dhal mixture into this pan, add the vegetables and chillies and simmer until vegetables are cooked.

Heat remaining tablespoon oil in small saucepan and fry the mustard seeds and sliced onion until seeds pop and onion is brown. Add to the soup, simmer a few minutes longer and serve. Sambar should be fairly thick, with a pronounced sour and hot flavour. Serve with rice, or thosai (page 11).

Amti

Lentil Soup with Coconut (Maharashtra)   *Serves: 6*

¾ cup toor dhal or split peas
  (mattar ki dhal)
½ teaspoon ground turmeric
8 cups water
1½ teaspoons salt
1 cup hot water
1 tablespoon tamarind pulp or
  1 teaspoon instant tamarind
2 teaspoons brown sugar or
  jaggery
1 tablespoon ghee or oil
½ teaspoon black mustard seeds
8 curry leaves
3 fresh green chillies, seeded
  and chopped
1 teaspoon crushed garlic
2 tablespoons desiccated
  coconut

Garnish:
1 tablespoon chopped fresh
  coriander, optional

Wash dhal well and put into a saucepan with the turmeric and 8 cups water. Bring to the boil, cover and cook until dhal is very soft, about 1 hour. If water reduces to less than 5 cups, add more. Add salt. Pour 1 cup hot water over tamarind pulp, leave to soak for 5 minutes, then squeeze to dissolve the pulp or stir instant tamarind into water until dissolved. Strain liquid into the boiling dhal mixture and discard seeds and fibres. Add sugar or jaggery.

In another saucepan heat ghee or oil and fry the mustard seeds, curry leaves and chillies until the mustard seeds pop. Add the garlic and stir for 1 minute or until garlic is golden. Add the coconut and the dhal mixture and simmer another 5 minutes. Sprinkle with the fresh coriander (if used) and serve hot as a soup or as an accompaniment to rice and curry.

Dhal Mulegoo Thani
Lentil Mulligatawny (South India)   *Serves: 4–5*

1 cup red lentils (masoor dhal)
2 medium onions
1 teaspoon sliced garlic
1 small stick cinnamon
¼ teaspoon whole black
    peppercorns
2 bay leaves
6 cups water

1 tablespoon ghee or oil
6–8 curry leaves
2 teaspoons salt
½ teaspoon garam masala
    (page xxx)
1 cup coconut milk, optional
    (page xxxv)

Wash the lentils well and leave to soak for about an hour. Drain, put
into a saucepan with 1 onion and ½ teaspoon garlic, the cinnamon,
peppercorns and bay leaves. Add water and bring to the boil. Cover
and simmer until lentils and onion are soft. Strain through a sieve,
puréeing the lentils and discarding the spices.

Slice remaining onion very thinly. Heat ghee or oil in saucepan
and fry the onion and curry leaves until onion is dark brown. Add
the lentil liquid, salt and garam masala and simmer for a minute or
two. If a richer soup is preferred, add the coconut milk at the end
and stir until it heats through.

Chaman
Fresh Cheese in Tomato Sauce (Kashmir)   *Serves: 4*

375 g (12 oz) ricotta cheese or
    panir (page xxiii)
2 tablespoons ghee
2 tablespoons oil
500 g (1 lb) ripe tomatoes
1 teaspoon ground turmeric
1 teaspoon chilli powder

1 medium onion, finely chopped
3 whole cloves
3 cardamom pods, bruised
¾ teaspoon salt
1 tablespoon sugar or to taste
pinch of saffron strands
2 tablespoons hot water

Cut the cheese in slices abut 1 cm (½ inch) thick and fry in ghee and
oil until golden. Put on a plate and set aside. Add peeled and
chopped tomatoes, spices, salt and sugar and cook until gravy is
thick, adding the slices of cheese and allowing them to simmer in
the gravy. Dissolve saffron in hot water and add about 5 minutes
before end of cooking. Serve with rice or chapatis.

Dhal
Lentil Purée   *Serves: 4–6*

1 cup red lentils (masoor dhal)
1½ tablespoons ghee or oil
1 large onion, finely sliced
1 teaspoon finely chopped garlic
1 teaspoon finely grated fresh
    ginger

½ teaspoon ground turmeric
3 cups hot water
1 teaspoon salt, or to taste
½ teaspoon garam masala
    (page xxx)

Any type of lentils can be used for this, but red lentils (masoor dhal) or moong dhal are the quickest cooking types and do not need soaking. Other types of lentils should be soaked overnight before cooking.

Wash lentils thoroughly, removing those that float on the surface. Drain well. Heat ghee or oil in saucepan and fry onion, garlic and ginger until onion is golden brown. Add turmeric and stir well. Add drained lentils and fry for a minute or two. Add hot water, bring to the boil, then reduce heat to simmer. Cover and cook for 15 to 20 minutes or until lentils are half cooked. Add salt and garam masala, mix well and continue cooking until lentils are soft and the consistency is similar to porridge. If there is too much liquid, leave the lid off the pan to speed evaporation. Serve dhal plain or garnished with sliced onions, fried until deep golden brown. Eat with boiled rice, Indian breads, or as a light meal by itself.

Karhi
Buttermilk Curry (Maharashtra)   *Serves: 4*

2½ cups buttermilk
2 tablespoons besan (chick pea
    flour)
½ cup cold water
1 teaspoon ground turmeric
1 teaspoon sugar
1 teaspoon salt
2 sprigs fresh coriander

2 fresh green chillies, seeded
1 tablespoon ghee or oil
1 teaspoon cummin seeds
½ teaspoon black mustard
    seeds
2 dried red chillies
⅛ teaspoon ground asafoetida,
    optional

Pour buttermilk into a saucepan and add to it the besan mixed to a smooth cream with cold water. Add turmeric, sugar and salt and mix well. Finely chop the coriander and green chillies or blend in electric blender with a little water.

Bring the buttermilk mixture to the boil over low heat, stirring constantly. Add the coriander and chilli and cook for 5 minutes, stirring. In a small pan heat the ghee or oil and fry the cummin and mustard seeds, the red chillies (broken in pieces and the seeds shaken out) and the asafoetida (if used). Stir into the buttermilk mixture and serve with rice or as a soup.

Dahi Bhalas
Lentil Cakes in Yoghurt (Punjab)   *Serves: 6*

1½ cups urad dhal
1½ teaspoons salt
½ teaspoon finely grated fresh
   ginger, optional
pinch asafoetida, optional
oil or ghee for deep frying
1 cup yoghurt

1 cup buttermilk
1 teaspoon cummin seeds
½ teaspoon chilli powder
2 tablespoons chopped fresh
   coriander
1 fresh green chilli, seeded and
   chopped

I have heard these lentil cakes called 'badas', 'boras' and other names, but since the Punjabi lady who taught me how to make them calls them 'bhalas' I have used this word.

Wash urad dhal thoroughly in several changes of water, then soak in cold water overnight. Drain well, put into electric blender and blend at high speed, adding only as much water as is necessary to facilitate blending. It should form a thick, smooth paste. Add 1 teaspoon salt. Add finely grated fresh ginger and a pinch of asafoetida to the dhal if liked. With wet hands form mixture into flat patties about 5 cm (2 inches) across, and as each one is made drop it into hot oil or ghee. Fry, turning with slotted spoon, until pale golden—do not allow bhalas to brown. Drain on absorbent paper and when cool immerse in cold water for about 10 minutes. Press out excess moisture gently between palms, taking care not to break them.

Combine yoghurt, buttermilk and ½ teaspoon salt. Immerse the bhalas in this mixture and chill thoroughly. Roast the cummin seeds in a dry pan, stirring constantly until dark brown. Crush and sprinkle over the dish together with chilli powder, chopped coriander and fresh chilli. Serve cold as an accompaniment to rice or parathas.

Lobia
Savoury Black-Eyed Beans (Punjab)   *Serves: 4*

1 cup black-eyed beans
3 bay leaves
2 cardamom pods, bruised
2 teaspoons chopped garlic
½ teaspoon ground turmeric
1 teaspoon salt
2 medium onions, roughly
   chopped
2 teaspoons chopped fresh
   ginger
2 dried red chillies, seeded
2 tablespoons oil or ghee
1 teaspoon ground cummin
½ cup yoghurt
½ teaspoon garam masala
   (page xxx)

Garnish:
2 tablespoons chopped fresh
   coriander

Wash beans well and soak overnight in cold water to cover. Drain, cover with fresh water and bring to the boil with the bay leaves, cardamoms, 1 teaspoon chopped garlic, turmeric and salt. Cover and simmer until tender, or pressure-cook for about 15 minutes. Drain, reserving liquid.

Put the onions, remaining teaspoon garlic, ginger and chillies in blender and blend to a purée. Heat oil or ghee and fry the blended mixture, stirring. When it begins to brown add the cummin and fry, stirring, for a few seconds longer. Add the drained beans and the yoghurt blended with ½ cup of the liquid in which the beans cooked. Cook for a further 5 minutes or until the gravy thickens. Sprinkle with garam masala and coriander and serve with chapatis or rice.

Cholé
Savoury Chick Peas (Punjab)   *Serves: 4*

1 cup dried chick peas
  (kabuli channa)
2 teaspoons salt
2 bay leaves
2 tablespoons ghee or oil
2 large onions, finely chopped
2 teaspoons chopped garlic
2 teaspoons finely chopped
  fresh ginger
½ teaspoon ground turmeric

1 teaspoon garam masala
  (page xxx)
2 large ripe tomatoes, peeled
  and chopped
1 fresh green chilli, seeded and
  sliced
2 tablespoons chopped fresh
  mint or coriander
lemon juice to taste

Soak chick peas in cold water to cover overnight, or better still, for 24 hours. Drain, rinse and put the chick peas with just enough water to cover in a pressure cooker or heavy saucepan. Add salt and bay leaves and cook until just tender, about 20 minutes in pressure cooker. Drain, reserving liquid.

Heat ghee or oil in a heavy saucepan and fry the onion, garlic and ginger until golden, stirring frequently. Add turmeric and fry for a few seconds. Add the garam masala, tomatoes, chilli and half the fresh herbs. Add peas and stir well, then add the reserved cooking liquid, cover and simmer on low heat until peas are quite tender and the tomatoes have become a purée. Add lemon juice to taste and sprinkle with remaining fresh herbs. Serve with bhatura, a deep fried bread (page 37).

Fish and Shellfish

Fish in India is never, it seems, plain poached, steamed, baked or boiled. It is fried, but even then there are simple things done to it first that make a simply marvellous difference.

It doesn't take long to rub a slice of fish with ground turmeric and salt. Or to coat it in a mixture of *besan*, salt and spices. But when this is done, fried fish is more than just fish which has been fried.

When fish is baked, it is with a stuffing or coating of ground masalas and when it is boiled, it is always in a flavoursome liquid with spices so it qualifies as curry.

There are fish curries of many kinds—the rich red curries of Bengal, cooked in mustard oil; gently spiced kormas with yoghurt as in *machchi korma* from Punjab. Kerala and other coastal areas like to cook fish in coconut milk with plenty of hot chillies and a pronounced acid flavour from local fruits or vinegar.

A complete contrast is another Kerala speciality that has gained popularity elsewhere, *machchi molee*, a very mild curry with fish cooked in coconut milk without any of the hot spices. It is delicate and delicious.

Jhinga masala, king prawns fried with a mixture of spices and hot chillies, is a famous Goan preparation. It was in Panjim, capital of Goa, that we ate tiny sprats rubbed with spice and fried until even the bones were crisp. And another day in Panjim a good Portuguese cook prepared *fish balchao*, a sort of pickle-cum-curry which was memorable. Yes, Goa was a great place for seafood. At Fort Aguada, the beautiful beach resort, I met a talented and generous chef, José Gomes, who shared the secrets of his kitchen and cooked for us in a variety of ways the crabs, prawns and fish which abound in these parts.

A Maharashtrian speciality is fish (preferably pomfret) stuffed with a fresh chutney of ground coconut, fresh coriander, garlic and chillies and then grilled or fried. Variations of this theme appear in other regions too.

Jhinga patia, a Parsi prawn dish from Maharashtra is certainly worth trying for its spiciness and delightful sweet-sour flavours—but don't expect anything like a Chinese style sweet-sour dish, it is completely different.

Tandoori cooking, which has traditionally been only for meat, chicken and bread, is now being used for fish. At Temple Bay near the coastal village of Mahabalipuram I was served whole fish marinated with spices and cooked in the *tandoor* which left me eager to come home and try the recipe myself. It was superb, even if the *tandoor* had to be replaced with a barbecue or grill.

Along the coasts of South India a lot of fish is salted or dried and this is used during the monsoon months when it is too dangerous for the fishing boats to venture out.

Curry made from this fish is necessarily pungent, and salted fish is also very popular cooked as a pickle with lots of tamarind pulp, ginger, garlic and chillies. Perhaps the most widely known dried fish is Bombay duck, which is not a duck at all, but a long, narrow fish plentiful in the sea around Bombay. It is served as an accompaniment, in small pieces for it is very salty and strong flavoured. The texture is crisp and crumbly when it is deep fried, but it is also grilled or made into a pickle-curry. Treat it as a flavour accent rather than a main dish.

Bhangra Chatni

Grilled Mackerel with Green Chutney (Goa)　　　　　*Serves: 4*

4 small mackerel, about 375 g
　(12 oz) each, or other small fish
coarse salt
1 cup fresh grated or desiccated
　coconut
¾ cup chopped fresh coriander
1 small onion, chopped
2 teaspoons chopped garlic
pinch of ground cummin
6 large green chillies, seeded
　and chopped
2 teaspoons lemon juice
½ teaspoon sugar
1 teaspoon salt

Garnish:
fresh lime

Buy fish gutted and cleaned but with head left on. Scrub cavity with damp kitchen paper dipped in coarse salt and rinse well. With a sharp knife separate flesh from centre bone to make a pocket for the green chutney. Score the fish three or four times on each side. Rub over with salt.

If desiccated coconut is used, sprinkle with a little water and mix lightly with fingertips to moisten all the coconut evenly. Put all the ingredients except fish into electric blender and make green chutney by blending to a smooth paste. If necessary, add a little water to facilitate blending. In India these ingredients would be ground on a stone, resulting in a very thick paste, so use only as much water as is necessary.

Fill the pockets and cavities with the green chutney and grill the fish over coals or under a preheated grill. Garnish with wedges of fresh lime. Serve hot with rice.

Fish Balchao

Fish Pickle-Curry (Goa)   *Serves: 4*

10–12 dried red chillies,
  preferably Goan or Kashmiri
  type
500 g (1 lb) cutlets of firm fish
  such as halibut
1 teaspoon ground turmeric
1 teaspoon salt
6 tablespoons oil

3 teaspoons chopped garlic
2 teaspoons chopped fresh
  ginger
½ cup white vinegar
2 teaspoons ground cummin
1 teaspoon shrimp paste or
  bagoong

In Goa a special prawn masala made from a tiny variety of dried shrimps is used in balchao. I have substituted the more readily available Chinese shrimp paste or Filipino bagoong which are also made from shrimp and have a similar flavour.

Soak chillies in hot water to cover for 10 minutes. Wash and dry fish cutlets and rub over with turmeric and salt. Heat oil in frying pan and fry the fish until golden brown on both sides. Remove from pan and set aside.

In electric blender purée the onions, garlic, ginger, the drained chillies and vinegar until finely ground. Mix in ground cummin and shrimp paste or bagoong.

In the same pan in which fish was fried (add a little more oil if necessary) fry the blended mixture until dark in colour and oil shows around the edges. Stir constantly while frying. Add fish, cover and cook for about 8 minutes or until fish is cooked through. Serve with rice and curries.

Machchi Jhol
Bengal Fish Curry (Bengal)

Serves: 4

500 g (1 lb) fish fillets or a
  whole fish
1 teaspoon salt
2 teaspoons ground turmeric
4 dried red chillies, seeded
1 teaspoon chopped fresh
  ginger
1 cup yoghurt, beaten until
  smooth
2 tablespoons ghee

2 tablespoons mustard oil
2 bay leaves
1 onion, thinly sliced
4 fresh green chillies, split
  lengthways
1 teaspoon garam masala
  (page xxx)
2 tablespoons chopped fresh
  coriander

Cut the fish into large pieces, or use a medium-sized fish whole. Rub
fish with salt and turmeric. Soak the dried chillies in a little very hot
water for 10 minutes, then put into electric blender together with
the ginger and blend to a fine paste. Use yoghurt to facilitate
blending. Pour this marinade over the fish.

Heat ghee and oil in a saucepan, add the bay leaves, onion and
fresh chillies and fry until onion starts to turn brown. Add fish and
all the marinade, sprinkle with garam masala. Cover and simmer for
10 minutes, sprinkle with coriander and serve with rice.

Machchi Kari
Fish Curry with Coconut (Goa)

Serves: 6

750 g (1½ lb) fish steaks
lemon juice, salt and pepper
6 large dried red chillies,
  preferably Goan or Kashmiri
  type
2 tablespoons desiccated
  coconut
1 tablespoon coriander seeds
2 teaspoons cummin seeds
¼ teaspoon fenugreek seeds
4 teaspoons finely chopped
  garlic

1 teaspoon finely chopped fresh
  ginger
1 tablespoon tamarind pulp or
  1 teaspoon instant tamarind
½ cup hot water
2 tablespoons ghee or oil
1 large onion, finely chopped
1½ cups coconut milk
1½ teaspoons salt

Wash fish, rub over with lemon juice, salt and pepper and set aside. Soak the chillies in hot water for 10 minutes.

In a dry pan roast the coconut, stirring constantly, until brown. Remove coconut to a plate and dry roast the coriander, cummin and fenugreek seeds, shaking pan or stirring, until brown. Remove chillies from water and put together with coconut, spices, garlic and ginger into electric blender and blend to a smooth paste, adding a little water if necessary.

Soak tamarind pulp in hot water, squeeze to dissolve, strain. Alternatively dissolve instant tamarind in water. Heat ghee or oil in a heavy saucepan and fry the onion until soft. Add the blended mixture and fry on medium heat, stirring until it darkens in colour and smells cooked. Add the coconut milk, salt, tamarind liquid and bring slowly to simmering point, stirring to prevent curdling. Add the fish and simmer until fish is cooked. Do not cover. Serve hot with rice.

Note: Ground coriander, cummin and fenugreek may be used instead of whole seeds, but roast them on low heat, stirring constantly and taking care that they do not burn.

Machchi Khattai
Piquant Fish Curry (Bengal)   *Serves: 4*

750 g (1½ lb) fish steaks or fillets
1 tablespoon tamarind pulp or
  1 teaspoon instant tamarind
1 cup hot water
3 tablespoons oil or ghee
1 teaspoon black mustard
  seeds
½ teaspoon fenugreek seeds

1 medium onion, finely chopped
2 teaspoons finely chopped
  garlic
2 teaspoons finely grated fresh
  ginger
½ teaspoon ground turmeric
2 teaspoons ground cummin
2 teaspoons salt

Wash the fish, cut into serving pieces and set aside. Soak tamarind pulp in hot water, squeeze to dissolve, strain. Alternatively dissolve instant tamarind in water.

Heat the oil or ghee in a heavy saucepan and fry the mustard seeds until they pop. Add the fenugreek seeds, onion, garlic and ginger and fry, stirring, until the onion is soft and golden. Add the turmeric and cummin and stir for 1 minute, then add the salt and the strained tamarind liquid. Bring to the boil, add the fish and cook on low heat until fish is cooked. Serve with rice.

Machchi Do Piaza
Curried Fish (Bengal)   *Serves: 4–5*

500 g (1 lb) firm white fish
fillets
2 teaspoons ground turmeric
lemon juice
1½ teaspoons chilli powder
1 tablespoon chopped fresh
ginger
2 teaspoons chopped garlic

2 ripe tomatoes, chopped
2 large onions
¼ cup mustard oil or other
vegetable oil
4 fresh green chillies, seeded
and sliced
1 teaspoon salt
½ cup water

Wash fish, rub over with half the turmeric and lemon juice and set aside. Put remaining turmeric, chilli powder, ginger, garlic, tomatoes and one roughly chopped onion into electric blender and blend to a purée. Slice remaining onion very finely.

Heat mustard oil in a saucepan and fry the sliced onion, stirring frequently, until it is golden. Remove onion from pan and reserve. To the oil in the pan add the blended mixture and the sliced chillies. Stir over medium heat until the colour darkens and the oil separates from the mass. Add the fish, salt and water and simmer, covered, for about 15 minutes. Shake pan from time to time. This is safer than stirring, which could break up a delicate fish. Add the fried onions for the last five minutes of cooking. Serve with rice.

Tali Machchi
Fried Fish (Punjab)   *Serves: 4*

500 g (1 lb) firm white fish fillets
½ cup besan (chick pea flour)
½ cup atta (fine wholemeal
flour)
2 teaspoons salt
½ teaspoon ground black
pepper

½ teaspoon ground turmeric
1 teaspoon garam masala
(page xxx)
1 egg, well beaten
oil for deep frying

Wash and dry fish fillets and remove skin by holding fish skin side down against chopping board and using a very sharp knife.

Mix together the besan and atta flours, salt, pepper, turmeric and garam masala. Dip fish fillets into beaten egg, then coat with the flour mixture, pressing firmly with palm and then dusting off excess. Heat oil in a large karahi or frying pan and fry the fish quickly until golden brown on both sides. Lift out with a slotted spoon and drain on absorbent paper. Serve warm.

Masaladar Machchi
Marinated Fried Fish (Bengal)   *Serves: 4–6*

750 g (1½ lb) fish fillets
2 medium onions
1 teaspoon chopped garlic
1½ teaspoons chopped fresh ginger
2 fresh green chillies, seeded and chopped
1 small ripe tomato, peeled and chopped
¼ teaspoon ground black pepper
2 tablespoons salt
½ teaspoon ground turmeric

2 tablespoons lemon juice
½ cup plain flour or besan (chick pea flour)
½ cup sesame seeds
1 teaspoon paprika
1 egg, beaten
oil for frying
1 tablespoon ghee
6 curry leaves
3 cardamom pods, bruised
1 small stick cinnamon
¾ cup yoghurt

Wash fish, remove skin, cut into serving pieces and place in a single layer in a large dish. Put 1 onion, roughly chopped, garlic, ginger, chillies and tomato into electric blender and blend to a purée. Mix in pepper, 1 teaspoon salt, turmeric and lemon juice. Pour over dish, turning pieces in the marinade. Leave for 30 minutes or longer.

Combine flour with sesame seeds, remaining teaspoon of salt and paprika. Drain fish from marinade, reserving the marinade. Dip the pieces of fish in beaten egg and then in the flour mixture, making sure fish is coated on all surfaces. Heat oil in a frying pan, using enough to cover base of pan. When oil is hot fry the pieces of fish briefly, a few at a time, until golden brown on both sides. Remove from oil with slotted spoon and drain on absorbent paper.

Pour off all but 1 tablespoon of oil from pan. Add ghee to pan and fry the curry leaves, cardamom, cinnamon and remaining onion, finely sliced, until onion is golden. Add reserved marinade, stir and cook for a few minutes, then stir in yoghurt. Lay fish pieces in this mixture and simmer gently, uncovered, for 5 minutes. Serve with the sauce spooned over and accompanied by rice or chapatis.

Machchi Korma
Braised Fish with Saffron and Yoghurt (Punjab)   *Serves: 4–6*

750 g.(1½ lb) fish fillets
lemon juice
1 teaspoon salt
1 teaspoon ground black pepper
1 teaspoon ground turmeric
oil for frying
1 large onion, finely sliced
1 medium onion, roughly
  chopped
1 teaspoon chopped garlic
1 tablespoon chopped fresh
  ginger
2 or 3 fresh red chillies, seeded
2 tablespoons blanched almonds

1 tablespoon white poppy seeds,
  optional
2 teaspoons ground cummin
2 teaspoons ground coriander
¼ teaspoon ground cardamom
¼ teaspoon ground cinnamon
small pinch ground cloves
¼ cup cold water
¼ teaspoon saffron strands
2 tablespoons boiling water
½ cup yoghurt
salt to taste
2 tablespoons chopped fresh
  coriander

Wash and dry fish, cut into large serving pieces and rub with lemon juice, salt, pepper and turmeric. Heat oil in a frying pan for shallow frying and on high heat brown the fish quickly on both sides. Lift out onto a plate. In the same oil fry finely sliced onion until golden brown, remove and set aside. Put roughly chopped onion, garlic, ginger, chillies, almonds, poppy seeds (if used) into electric blender and purée. If necessary add a little water. Add ground spices and blend once again, briefly.

Pour off all but about 2 tablespoons oil from pan and fry the blended mixture until colour changes and it gives out a pleasing aroma. The mixture should be stirred constantly while frying and care taken that it does not stick to pan and burn. Add ¼ cup water to blender container and swirl out any remaining spice mixture. Add to pan.

Pound saffron strands in mortar and pestle, add boiling water and stir, add to mixture in pan. Add yoghurt, stir and simmer gently for a few minutes, then add fish pieces, turning them carefully in the sauce. Add salt to taste. Cover and simmer for about 10 minutes, then sprinkle with coriander and serve hot with rice.

Machchi Sas
Fish in Sweet-Sour Sauce (Maharashtra Parsi)   *Serves: 4*

500 g (1 lb) fish steaks or fillets
lemon juice
1 teaspoon salt
2 tablespoons ghee or oil
1 large onion, finely sliced
1 fresh red and 1 fresh green
   chilli, seeded and sliced
1 teaspoon finely chopped garlic
1/4 teaspoon ground black
   pepper
1 large or 2 small eggs
2 teaspoons sugar
1/2 cup white vinegar
1 teaspoon cummin seeds

Garnish:
1 tablespoon chopped fresh
   coriander

Wash and dry the fish, rub over with lemon juice and salt. Heat ghee or oil and fry the onion, chillies and garlic over low heat until soft and golden, stirring occasionally. Add the fish to the pan in one layer, sprinkle with half the pepper, and cook, covered, for 5 minutes. Turn pieces over, sprinkle with more pepper, cover and cook for a further 5 minutes. Remove fish from pan, arrange on serving plate and keep warm.

Beat eggs and mix in the sugar and vinegar. To onion mixture in pan add the beaten egg mixture, keeping heat very low and stirring constantly. Take care that it does not boil as the sauce will curdle. When thickened, spoon sauce over the fish. Roast cummin seeds in a dry pan, stirring constantly until dark brown. Grind with pestle and mortar. Sprinkle ground cummin over dish and garnish with coriander leaves. Serve hot, accompanied by rice.

Machchi Molee

Fish in Coconut Milk (Kerala)   *Serves: 4–6*

750 g (1½ lb) fish fillets or steaks
lemon juice
1 teaspoon ground turmeric
1½ teaspoons salt
2 tablespoons oil or ghee
2 small onions, finely sliced
2 teaspoons finely sliced garlic
3 slices fresh ginger, cut into
   slivers

8–10 curry leaves
3 fresh green chillies, seeded
   and cut in half lengthways
2 cups thin coconut milk
   (page xxxv)
1 cup thick coconut milk
   (page xxxv)
lime or lemon juice to taste
salt to taste

Wash the fish and rub over with lemon juice, turmeric and salt.

Heat the oil or ghee in a saucepan and on low heat fry the onions, garlic, ginger, curry leaves and chillies until onions are soft. Stir frequently and do not allow any of the ingredients to brown. Add the thin coconut milk and stir while it comes to simmering point. Add the fish and cook slowly, uncovered, for 10 minutes. Add thick coconut milk, stir gently, heat through and remove from heat, then add lime or lemon juice and salt to taste. Serve with white rice and nariyal chatni (page 140).

Tandoori Machchi

Barbecued Fish (North India)   *Serves: 4*

1 whole fish, about 1 kg (2 lb)
coarse salt
2 teaspoons crushed garlic
2 teaspoons finely grated fresh
   ginger
1½ teaspoons salt
1 teaspoon ground cummin
1 teaspoon chilli powder

1 teaspoon ground turmeric
pinch red food colouring
   powder or 2 teaspoons
   paprika
approximately 2 tablespoons
   lemon juice
3 tablespoons melted ghee
2 teaspoons garam masala
   (page xxx)

For this recipe use mullet, halibut or other firm fish.

Buy fish cleaned and scaled with head removed. Clean the cavity of the fish with several pieces of kitchen paper dampened and dipped in coarse salt. Wash the fish well under cold running water, then blot dry with kitchen paper. With a sharp knife cut slashes on each side of the fish, almost to the bone. Combine the garlic, ginger, salt, cummin, chilli powder, turmeric and colouring powder or paprika. This is what gives tandoori fish its distinctive colour. Add enough lemon juice to form a thick paste.

Rub the marinade all over the fish, inside and out and leave for 1 hour or longer in the refrigerator.

Pass a long metal skewer through the fish from head to tail and cook over glowing coals, or under preheated grill, brushing with the melted ghee. It should take 6 or 7 minutes cooking on each side. When fish is almost cooked, sprinkle with garam masala. Serve with naan, parathas or puris.

Kakra Kalia

Crab Curry (Bengal)   *Serves: 4–6*

2 or 3 medium-sized crabs
3 tablespoons oil or ghee
2 medium onions, finely
  chopped
2 teaspoons finely grated garlic
2 teaspoons finely grated fresh
  ginger
2 bay leaves
2 fresh red chillies, seeded and
  sliced

2 teaspoons ground coriander
2 teaspoons ground cummin
2 tablespoons ground almonds
  or white poppy seeds
1½ teaspoons salt or to taste
1 cup tomato purée
1½ cups coconut milk
  (page xxxv)
3 tablespoons chopped fresh
  coriander

Remove large shells of crabs and discard all fibrous tissue found under the shell. Divide each crab into 4 portions, breaking the body in half and separating the large, meaty claws from the body. Legs should be left attached to the body.

Heat the oil or ghee in a large saucepan and fry the onions, garlic, ginger, bay leaves and chillies until onions are soft and golden. Add ground coriander, cummin and ground almonds or poppy seeds and fry for a minute or so longer. Then add the salt, tomato purée and coconut milk and stir while bringing to a gentle simmer.

Put in the crabs and cook, uncovered, for 15–20 minutes or until the crabs are done. If pan is not large enough, cook in two lots. When cooked the shells will turn bright red and the flesh become white and opaque. If cooked crabs are used, reduce cooking time by half. Add fresh coriander during last 5 minutes. Serve with plain boiled rice.

Jhinga Masala
Masala King Prawns (Goa)   *Serves 4–6*

750 g (1½ lb) raw king prawns
8–10 dried red chillies
2 teaspoons chopped fresh
   ginger
2 teaspoons chopped garlic
½ teaspoon ground cinnamon
¼ teaspoon ground black
   pepper
¼ teaspoon ground cloves
1 teaspoon ground cummin

½ teaspoon ground turmeric
¼ cup vinegar
⅓ cup oil
3 medium onions, finely sliced
1 green pepper, sliced
3 ripe tomatoes, peeled and
   chopped
2 tablespoons lemon juice
1½ teaspoons salt or to taste

Wash prawns and drain but do not remove shells or heads. Soak chillies in hot water for 5 minutes. Put ginger, garlic, chillies and a little water into electric blender and blend on high speed until smooth. Mix in the spices and vinegar.

Heat oil and fry the onions and pepper until soft. Add prawns and fry on high heat, stirring, just until they change colour, then add the blended mixture and fry for about 5 minutes, stirring. Add tomatoes, lemon juice and salt. Simmer, covered, for 10 minutes.

Jhinga Patia
Sweet-Sour Prawns (Maharashtra Parsi)   *Serves: 4*

500 g (1 lb) raw prawns
1 teaspoon salt
1 teaspoon ground turmeric
2 teaspoons chilli powder, or
   to taste
6 fresh green chillies
2 teaspoons chopped garlic
1½ teaspoons chopped fresh
   ginger
3 teaspoons cummin seeds
5 tablespoons light sesame oil

3 medium onions, sliced thinly
2 ripe tomatoes, peeled and
   chopped
4 tablespoons chopped fresh
   coriander
1 teaspoon jaggery or brown
   sugar
1 tablespoon tamarind pulp or
   1 teaspoon instant tamarind
½ cup hot water

Shell and de-vein the prawns. Sprinkle with salt, turmeric and chilli powder and set aside.

Grind together in blender two seeded chillies, garlic, ginger and cummin, adding a little oil if necessary to facilitate blending.

Heat oil in a saucepan and fry the remaining whole chillies and remove. Fry the onions over medium heat, stirring occasionally, until golden. Add the blended spices and cook, stirring, for a few minutes. Add tomatoes and half the coriander. Add prawns and cook for 10 minutes. Dissolve tamarind pulp in hot water and strain. Alternatively dissolve instant tamarind in hot water. Stir in tamarind liquid and jaggery or brown sugar. Serve garnished with fried green chillies and remaining coriander.

Jhinga Baffad
Prawns in Spicy Sauce (Goa)   *Serves: 4*

500 g (1 lb) raw prawns
4–6 dried red chillies
½ teaspoon cummin seeds
¼ teaspoon ground black pepper
1½ teaspoons chopped garlic
1 teaspoon chopped fresh ginger

1 teaspoon ground turmeric
3 tablespoons oil
2 medium onions, chopped
1 ripe tomato, chopped
1 teaspoon salt
vinegar to taste

Shell and de-vein prawns, rinse well and drain in colander. Discard seeds and stalks of chillies, and soak chillies in hot water for 5 minutes. Put chillies, cummin, pepper, garlic, ginger and turmeric into electric blender and blend at high speed, adding a little oil to facilitate blending. If blender is not available, substitute 2 teaspoons chilli powder for dried chillies, ground cummin for cummin seeds, and finely grate the garlic and ginger. Mix these ingredients together with the turmeric.

Heat oil and fry onions until soft and golden. Add blended mixture and fry for a few minutes, then add the tomato, salt and vinegar. Cover and cook until tomato is reduced to pulp. Add prawns, stir well, cover and cook until prawns are cooked, about 10 minutes. Serve with white rice.

Jhinga Vindaloo
Prawn Vindaloo (Goa)   *Serves: 4*

500 g (1 lb) large raw prawns
2 medium onions, roughly
  chopped
2 teaspoons chopped garlic
2 fresh red or green chillies,
  chopped
2 teaspoons chopped fresh
  ginger
¼ cup white vinegar

1½ teaspoons ground cummin
1 teaspoon garam masala
  (page xxx)
1 teaspoon ground turmeric
1 teaspoon salt
4 tablespoons oil
1 large onion, finely sliced
3 tablespoons lemon juice

Shell and de-vein prawns, wash and drain well. Put chopped onions, garlic, chillies, ginger and vinegar in electric blender and grind to a pulp. If blender is not available crush the garlic, grate ginger finely and chop onions very fine. Add ground cummin and garam masala, half the turmeric and salt. Rub remaining turmeric and salt over the prawns.

Heat oil in a saucepan and fry the sliced onion until soft and turning brown. Add the blended mixture and fry, stirring, until it is well cooked and oil separates from the mass. Add the prawns, bring to a slow simmer and cook for 8–10 minutes. Stir in lemon juice and serve with rice.

Chingri Malai Kari
Prawn Curry with Cream (Bengal)   *Serves: 4*

500 g (1 lb) raw prawns
2 large onions
2 fresh green chillies, seeded
1 teaspoon chopped garlic
1 teaspoon chopped fresh
  ginger
4 tablespoons oil

½ teaspoon black mustard seeds
½ teaspoon ground turmeric
1 teaspoon jaggery or brown
  sugar
1 cup coconut milk, (page xxxv)
½ cup cream
½ teaspoon garam masala
  (page xxx)

Shell and de-vein the prawns, rinse and drain. Slice one onion finely and set aside. Roughly chop the other onion and put into electric blender with the chillies, garlic and ginger. Blend to a smooth purée.

Heat oil in a saucepan and fry the black mustard seeds until they pop. Add the sliced onion and fry, stirring, until onion is soft but not brown. Add the turmeric and the blended mixture and fry, stirring, for about 5 minutes. Add the jaggery or sugar, and coconut milk and cream and bring to the boil, stirring. Simmer on low heat for 5 minutes, then add prawns, return to the boil and simmer for about 10 minutes just until prawns are cooked. Do not overcook. Sprinkle with garam masala. Serve with plain white rice or masala bhath (page 34).

Jhinga Kari
Hot Prawn Curry (Kerala)   *Serves: 6*

1 kg (2 lb) raw prawns in their shells
6 dried red chillies, preferably Kashmiri or Goan chillies
2 medium onions, chopped
3 teaspoons chopped garlic
3 teaspoons chopped fresh ginger
4 tablespoons oil

12 curry leaves
1 teaspoon ground turmeric
1 teaspoon ground coriander
1 teaspoon ground cummin
½ teaspoon ground fennel
2 teaspoons paprika
2 teaspoons salt
2½ cups coconut milk (page xxxv)
lemon juice to taste

A rich, red gravy based on coconut milk and chillies makes this quite a spicy dish but even if the quantity of chillies is reduced the curry still has good flavour.

Wash the prawns and remove hard shell from head but leave the legs and body shell on. Drain well. Soak the chillies (discard seeds if a very hot curry is not wanted) in hot water for 5 minutes and put into electric blender with the onion, garlic and ginger. Blend to a purée.

Heat oil in a heavy saucepan and fry the curry leaves for 1 or 2 minutes then add the blended mixture and fry, stirring constantly, for 5 minutes or until it smells cooked and the oil starts to separate around the edges. Add ground spices and fry for 1 minute, then add prawns and fry, stirring, until they change colour. Add the salt and coconut milk and simmer, uncovered, for 10 minutes. Remove from heat, add lemon juice to taste and serve with rice.

Jhinga Dhal
Prawn and Lentil Soup (South India)   *Serves: 4–6*

500 g (1 lb) small prawns
250g (8 oz) green beans
¾ cup red lentils
2 tablespoons oil
2 medium onions, finely sliced
1 teaspoon finely chopped
  garlic

1 teaspoon finely grated fresh
  ginger
2 fresh red or green chillies, split
1 teaspoon ground turmeric
4 cups water
1½ teaspoons salt
1 cup coconut milk, (page xxxv)
  optional
lemon juice to taste

Shell and de-vein the prawns. Top and tail beans, remove any strings and cut into thin diagonal slices. Wash the lentils well and drain.

In a saucepan heat oil and fry the onions over high heat, stirring until they are golden brown. Add the garlic and ginger and stir, then add the chillies and turmeric and fry for a few seconds longer. Add lentils and fry, stirring, for a minute or two, then add the water and allow it to come to the boil. Lower heat, cover and cook for 15 minutes. Add prawns, beans and salt and continue cooking until lentils are soft. Add the coconut milk or more water so the consistency is that of a soup. Add lemon juice, taste and add more salt if necessary. Serve with rice.

Chingri Kari
Prawn Mustard Curry (Bengal)   *Serves: 4*

500 g (1 lb) large raw prawns
4 dried red chillies, seeded
1 tablespoon black mustard
  seeds
3 medium onions, roughly
  chopped
2 teaspoons chopped garlic

½ teaspoon ground turmeric
¼ cup water
2 tablespoons oil
1 tablespoon ghee
8 dried curry leaves
1½ cups hot water
3 tablespoons lemon juice

Shell and de-vein prawns, rinse and drain. Soak dried chillies and mustard seeds in hot water for 5 minutes, then drain and put into electric blender with the cummin seeds, onions, garlic, turmeric and ¼ cup water. Blend to a purée.

Heat oil and ghee in a saucepan, fry the curry leaves for a few seconds, then add the blended mixture and fry, stirring, for 5 minutes or until the mixture smells cooked and the oil separates from the mass. Add $1\frac{1}{2}$ cups hot water, cover and simmer for 15 minutes. Add prawns, simmer 10 minutes, add lemon juice and serve with rice.

Poultry and Eggs

In India, chicken is reserved for special occasions. Prepared with the spices and flavours used by clever Indian cooks, it is surely a special treat.

There is seemingly no end to the ways in which chicken can be cooked. There is, of course, chicken curry – not just one curry but literally hundreds of different curries. Some curries are creamy with coconut milk, some rich with almonds and yoghurt, some hot with chillies, some piquant with tomatoes and some almost pickled, in the vindaloo style. Then there are other dishes besides curries – curry implying a dish with plenty of sauce. These include 'dry' dishes with superb flavour but not much gravy, which makes them ideal for eating with Indian breads. There are the famous *tandoori* dishes, *tikka kebab* (pieces of chicken marinated in spiced yoghurt, skewered and grilled) or *tandoori murgh*. The blending of spices in a marinade, the way the skin is removed so flavours can penetrate, the cooking in an earthen oven over fiercely hot coals, all contribute to this very special Indian dish. While it may not be possible for you to cook chicken in a *tandoor*, very convincing results are possible with the facilities in most Western kitchens, particularly with a rotisserie.

Many Indian recipes specify the cutting of chicken into 'curry pieces'. Cutting a chicken for curry is rather different from the way it is cut for Western dishes, the idea being to cut smaller pieces to allow for as much penetration of spices as possible.

First joint the chicken, then cut each thigh in two with a heavy cleaver. The breast is divided down the centre, then each half cut into 2 pieces. Wings are divided into two, cutting at the first joint and leaving the wing tip attached to the second joint. The back is cut into 4 pieces and used in curry, though these are not counted as serving pieces because there is very little meat on them. Neck and giblets are also used. This method may be used for all but the smallest chickens, for which it is unnecessary to cut the thighs in two.

Eggs are also special when cooked Indian style and the Parsis are just about the most lavish users of eggs among India's many different communities. They cook them superbly. You'll never be satisfied with plain old scrambled eggs or omelette once you've tasted them cooked Parsi style.

Strict vegetarians do not include eggs in their diet, though some do eat infertile eggs.

Murgh Khandan
Spicy Fried Chicken (Uttar Pradesh)   *Serves: 4*

1 x 1.25 kg (2½ lb) roasting
  chicken
1 teaspoon finely chopped
  garlic
1 teaspoon salt
1 teaspoon finely grated fresh
  ginger
1 teaspoon ground cardamom
½ teaspoon ground nutmeg
½ teaspoon ground black
  pepper
1 tablespoon ghee
2 tablespoons oil
1 fresh green chilli, seeded and
  chopped
½ cup roasted cashews, finely
  chopped or ground
  boiled cauliflower springs,
  carrot sticks, green peas or
  other vegetables

Garnish:
2 hard boiled eggs
2 firm red tomatoes

Wash and dry the chicken and cut into joints, separating
drumsticks from thighs and cutting breast in two lengthways. Put
chopped garlic on wooden board, sprinkle with salt and crush to a
smooth paste. Combine garlic, ginger, and ground spices and rub
this paste over the chicken pieces. Set aside for at least 30 minutes.

Heat ghee and oil in a heavy pan and brown the chicken pieces.
Add cashews and cook for a minute or two, then add about ¼ cup
water, cover and simmer on low heat until chicken is cooked, about
10 minutes. Put chicken pieces in serving dish, add boiled
vegetables to pan and toss in the spicy gravy. Arrange on serving
dish with chicken. Garnish with hard boiled eggs and tomatoes and
serve with rice or parathas.

Murgh Shaguti Masala
Chicken Shaguti (Maharashtra)   *Serves: 6*

1 x 1.5 kg (3 lb) roasting chicken
  or 2 kg (4 lb) duck
8 dried red chillies, preferably
  Kashmiri or Goan
1 tablespoon ground coriander
1 teaspoon ground cummin
½ teaspoon fenugreek seeds
8 whole black peppercorns
3 teaspoons white poppy seeds
½ cup desiccated coconut
1 large onion, finely sliced

1 teaspoon ground turmeric
½ teaspoon ground cardamom
¼ teaspoon ground cloves
½ teaspoon ground cinnamon
1 tablespoon ghee
2 tablespoons oil
2 teaspoons chopped garlic
2 teaspoons chopped ginger
2 teaspoons salt
½ cup hot water
juice of half a lemon

Shaguti (also spelt Saguti, Shagotti, Shakootee or even Xacuti) is a curry in which ingredients are roasted for dark colour and subtle changes in flavour, then ground to a thick, smooth paste. I tasted Chicken Shaguti in Maharashtra and Crab Xacuti in Goa, and while there may be minor changes in spice combinations, the common denominator is the rich masala which includes coconut and white poppy seeds. Also very successful with duck.

Cut chicken into curry pieces (page 89). Soak the chillies in hot water for 10 minutes. Meanwhile, roast coriander and cummin in a dry pan over medium heat, stirring constantly for a minute or two, until the colour changes and a pleasant aroma is given off. Turn onto a plate. Roast fenugreek seeds and peppercorns for 2 or 3 minutes, stirring constantly. In the same way roast the poppy seeds and the desiccated coconut, separately. Add to the other roasted spices. Put the sliced onion in the pan and dry roast, stirring, until brown.

Put chillies into electric blender with all roasted ingredients and the turmeric, cardamom, cloves and cinnamon. Add some of the water in which the chillies soaked and grind to a paste.

Heat ghee and oil in a heavy pan and fry the ground mixture and the garlic and ginger, stirring constantly, until oil separates from the mass. Put in the chicken, sprinkle with salt and stir to coat every piece of chicken with the mixture.

Add ½ cup hot water, cover and cook on very low heat, stirring occasionally and adding more water if necessary, until the chicken is tender. Add lemon juice when chicken is cooked. The gravy should be very thick and dark. Serve with rice and pickles.

Tandoori Murgh
Barbecued Chicken (North India)   *Serves: 4*

2 spring chickens, about 500 g
   (1 lb) each
¾ cup yoghurt
1½ teaspoons salt
1½ teaspoons crushed garlic
1½ teaspoons finely grated fresh
   ginger
½ teaspoon white pepper

½ teaspoon chilli powder
1 teaspoon garam masala
   (page xxx)
½ teaspoon ground fenugreek,
   optional
red food colour, optional
2 tablespoons ghee for oven
   method

Everyone has a slightly different recipe for tandoori chicken, but a few things remain the same in every version. One of the most important points is that the chicken should be a small one – spring chicken size – and that the skin should be removed to allow the full flavour of the marinade to penetrate the flesh. To be truly authentic it should, of course, be cooked in an earthen oven called a tandoor – where the heat is so intense that the chicken on its metal skewer is done in about 15 minutes – but where this is not possible, adapt the recipe to suit a barbecue, oven or grill. This version is from the Executive Chef of the Hotel Ashoka in Delhi.

With a sharp knife cut through the skin of the chickens right down the centre, front and back. Skin the chickens, then make slits in the flesh to allow spices to penetrate.

To make marinade combine yoghurt with all the other ingredients except ground fenugreek and ghee. Rub marinade all over and inside the chickens, and leave for 2–4 hours, or cover and refrigerate overnight.

If cooking on a barbecue, make sure fire has had time to burn down to glowing coals and cut chicken in halves lengthways. Place chickens on a rack above the coals and allow to cook until tender, turning the pieces so they cook on both sides.

If cooking in an oven, use hot oven preheated to 200°C (400°F). Melt 2 tablespoons ghee in a roasting pan, put the two chickens in the pan, side by side, breasts downwards. Spoon melted ghee over them and roast in oven for 20 minutes. Turn chickens on one side and roast for another 15 minutes, then turn them on the other side, baste again and roast for a further 15 minutes. For the final 10–15 minutes of browning, turn the chickens breast upwards and baste every 5 minutes. If oven has a rotisserie, cook the chicken on this. It will still be necessary to baste the chicken as the skin has been removed. Serve hot with parathas or naan and piaz sambal (page 137).

Note: If preferred substitute 3 teaspoons tandoori mix (page xxxi) for the pepper, chilli and garam masala in the marinade.

Murgh Dopiaza
Chicken Dopiaza (Uttar Pradesh)   *Serves: 6*

1 x 1.5 kg (3 lb) roasting chicken
6 medium onions
4 fresh green chillies, seeded
4 teaspoons chopped garlic
1½ tablespoons finely grated ginger
1 tablespoon ground coriander
1 tablespoon ground cummin
2 teaspoons ground turmeric
1 teaspoon ground cinnamon
1 teaspoon ground cardamom
¼ teaspoon ground cloves
3 tablespoons ghee
3 tablespoons oil
3 ripe tomatoes, peeled and chopped
1 cup water
3 teaspoons salt

This rich chicken curry is said to have been named for that famous philosopher and wit, Mullah Dopiaza. If more convenient, use two smaller chickens, or in families where everyone wants a drumstick, use an equivalent weight of drumsticks.

Cut chicken into curry pieces (page 89). Thinly slice half the onions and set aside. Roughly chop the rest of the onions and put into electric blender with the chillies, garlic and ginger. Blend to a purée. Mix in the ground spices. Heat ghee and oil in a large saucepan and fry the sliced onions, stirring frequently, until they are golden brown. Remove onions from pan with slotted spoon. Add the blended mixture to oil remaining in pan and fry, stirring until colour darkens and oil appears around the edges. Add tomatoes, stir and cook until liquid from tomatoes is almost evaporated. Add the chicken pieces and stir well. Add water and salt, cover and cook for 35 minutes or until chicken is tender. Add reserved fried onions, cover and simmer 5 minutes longer. Serve with rice or parathas.

Tikka Kebab
Chicken Kebabs (North India)   *Serves: 4*

1 kg (2 lb) chicken pieces, breast
   and thighs or 1 x 1.5 kg (3 lb)
   roasting chicken
1 small onion, roughly chopped
1 teaspoon chopped garlic
1 teaspoon chopped fresh
   ginger
1 tablespoon lemon juice
2 tablespoons yoghurt

1 teaspoon ground coriander
½ teaspoon ground cummin
1 teaspoon garam masala
   (page xxx)
1 teaspoon salt
1 tablespoon ground almonds
   or white poppy seeds

Bone chicken pieces and remove skin, or use meat from breast and thighs of roasting chicken. Cut meat into bite-size pieces.

Put onion, garlic, ginger and lemon juice into electric blender and blend until smooth. Mix in remaining ingredients and marinate chicken in this mixture for at least 2 hours, or overnight in the refrigerator. Thread chicken pieces on skewers and cook over glowing coals or under preheated grill. Serve with piaz sambal (page 137) and chapatis or naan.

Murgh Kaleja Kebab
Skewered Chicken Livers (North India)   *Serves: 4*

500 g (1 lb) chicken livers
1 medium onion
oil for frying
1 teaspoon crushed garlic
2 tablespoons yoghurt
1 teaspoon oil
1 teaspoon chilli powder or to
   taste
½ teaspoon brown sugar

½ teaspoon fragrant spice garam
   masala (page xxx) or
⅛ teaspoon each ground
   cinnamon, cloves, cardamom
   and nutmeg
1 tablespoon ground almonds or
   cashews
1 tablespoon white poppy seeds,
   optional
1 teaspoon salt

Wash the chicken livers and cut each in two. Bring a little lightly salted water to the boil, drop in the livers and leave for no more than 1 minute. This is not intended to cook the livers, but to firm them slightly. Drain well.

Slice half the onion finely and fry in oil until brown, cool and put into electric blender with remaining onion, roughly chopped, and all other ingredients except chicken livers and grind to a smooth paste. Marinate the chicken livers in the mixture for about 2 hours, then thread on bamboo skewers and cook over glowing coals or under preheated grill. Serve with rice.

Murgh Musallam

Spiced Roast Chicken (Kashmiri Moslem Style)　　　*Serves: 4–5*

1 x 1.5 kg (3 lb) roasting chicken
1 tablespoon ghee
½ cup water

Marinade:
1½ teaspoons ground dry
　ginger
2 teaspoons finely grated garlic
1 small onion, finely grated
1 teaspoon salt
1 teaspoon Kashmiri garam
　masala (page xxx)
2 teaspoons white poppy seeds,
　ground, optional
2 tablespoons yoghurt

Stuffing:
½ cup basmati or other long
　grain rice
1 tablespoon ghee
pinch of asafoetida, optional
½ teaspoon chilli powder or to
　taste
1 tablespoon blanched almonds
1 tablespoon chironji or
　pistachios
2 tablespoons sultanas
2 tablespoons khoa (page xxi)
½ teaspoon salt
¾ cup water

Fork the chicken so spice marinade can penetrate. Mix all the marinade ingredients together and rub all over chicken, inside as well as out. Set aside for 1 hour, or longer in the refrigerator.

Prepare the stuffing, allow to cool somewhat, fill cavity of the chicken, and fasten opening with small poultry skewers. Truss the chicken, tying legs together and tucking wings underneath.

Place chicken in a heavy saucepan with the ghee and ½ cup water, cover and cook on low heat until tender, about 1¼ hours. Turn chicken during cooking to allow browning on all sides. If preferred, finish by browning the chicken in a moderately hot oven, 190°C (375°F), for 15 minutes.

Stuffing: Wash rice well and soak for 1 hour in cold water, then drain well. Heat the ghee and fry the rice for a few minutes, stirring all the time. Add all other ingredients, cover and cook for 12–15 minutes.

Badami Murgh
Chicken Curry with One Hundred Almonds (North India) *Serves: 6*

1 x 1.5 kg (3 lb) roasting chicken
5 medium onions
2 tablespoons oil
2 tablespoons ghee
3 teaspoons finely chopped
  garlic
3 teaspoons finely grated fresh
  ginger
1 tablespoon ground coriander
1 tablespoon ground cummin
1 teaspoon ground turmeric
½ teaspoon ground fennel

1 teaspoon chilli powder,
  optional
3 teaspoons salt
3 large ripe tomatoes, peeled
  and chopped
¼ cup chopped fresh coriander
  or mint leaves
100 blanched almonds
oil for frying
1 cup yoghurt
1 teaspoon garam masala
  (page xxx)

Sometimes called 'hundred almond curry', a wonderfully extravagant-sounding name, sure to impress guests. The almonds are primarily to thicken the gravy so it may be scooped up on the flat chapatis or parathas which are the staple diet of Northern India; but almonds also add flavour and richness and shades of the Moghul Emperors and their days of splendour. Serve this curry with a pilau rice or parathas, fresh chutneys and raitas and you have a meal fit for a king.

Cut chicken into curry pieces (page 89). Peel onions, chop 3 onions finely and slice the remaining 2 very fine. Heat ghee and oil in a large heavy saucepan and fry the 2 sliced onions, stirring, until golden brown. Remove from pan and set aside. Add the chopped onion, garlic and ginger to the oil left in pan and fry on low heat, stirring occasionally, until very soft and turning golden. Long, slow cooking at this stage is essential if the curry is to have good flavour.

Add the coriander, cummin, turmeric, fennel and chilli powder and fry, stirring, for 1-2 minutes. Add salt, tomatoes and half the fresh herbs, stir well and cook until tomatoes are pulpy. Cover pan to hasten this process, but uncover and stir now and then to ensure mixture does not stick to base of pan.

Put in the chicken pieces and stir well so that each piece is coated with the mixture. Cover pan and cook on very low heat for 40 minutes or until chicken is tender. Meanwhile heat oil and fry half the almonds until golden. Grind remaining almonds. Beat the yoghurt with a fork until it is quite smooth and stir into the curry together with the fried almonds. Simmer for 5 minutes, uncovered. Stir in the garam masala, reserved fried onions, ground almonds and remaining chopped herbs. Heat through and serve.

Murgh Vindaloo
Chicken Vinegar Curry (Goa)   *Serves: 4–5*

1 x 1.5 kg (3 lb) roasting chicken
2 tablespoons cummin seed
1 tablespoon black mustard
  seeds
3 teaspoons chilli powder or to
  taste
1 tablespoon chopped ginger
1 tablespoon chopped garlic
½ cup vinegar

1 teaspoon ground cinnamon
¼ teaspoon ground cloves
¼ teaspoon ground cardamom
4 tablespoons oil
2 teaspoons salt
½ teaspoon ground black
  pepper

There are many versions of vindaloo, some containing onions, potatoes and eggs. This recipe, however, is one in which the accent is on ingredients which help preserve meat and the chicken is cooked with a lot of mustard and vinegar which more or less pickle the meat, though it is eaten as a curry.

Cut the chicken into small serving pieces, separating drumsticks from thighs and cutting breast into four. Grind the cummin seeds, mustard seeds, chilli (if used), ginger and garlic in electric blender with the vinegar. Use high speed so that mixture is finely ground. Add the ground spices.

Heat oil in a stainless steel or enamel saucepan, remove from heat and add the blended mixture to the hot oil. Stir for a few seconds, then add the chicken pieces and stir again so that each piece is coated with the spices. Let it stand for an hour or longer to marinate.

On low heat bring to simmering point, add salt and pepper and simmer, covered, until chicken is tender. Stir from time to time so that spices do not stick to the base of pan. Serve with plain white rice.

Moglai Murgh
Whole Chicken with Rice, Moghul Style (Kashmir)   *Serves: 4–5*

1 x 2 kg (4 lb) roasting chicken
2 tablespoons almonds
1 tablespoon chironji seeds or
    pistachios
2 tablespoons white poppy seeds
1 teaspoon caraway seeds
1 teaspoon cummin seeds
1 teaspoon chilli powder,
    optional
1 teaspoon ground coriander
½ teaspoon ground turmeric
½ teaspoon saffron strands
2 tablespoons boiling water
1 cup yoghurt
3½ teaspoons salt

3 hard boiled eggs
2 tablespoons ghee or oil
2 large onions, finely sliced
2 tablespoons finely chopped
    fresh coriander
1 tablespoon finely chopped
    fresh mint
2 or 3 fresh green chillies, seeded
    and chopped
1 cup hot water
2 cups basmati or other
    long grain rice
½ cup sultanas
½ cup green peas

Garnish:
silver leaf, optional
½ cup almonds or cashews, fried

Moghul court life was the inspiration of some rich and ostentatious dishes and court cooks were lavish in the use of ghee, almonds, pistachios, and threw in precious saffron as though it grew in the backyard, but then it did. Kashmir is still famous for its saffron, as it is one of the few places in the world where this costly spice grows. With sundry modifications, here is a dish that is exotic enough for the gourmet cook, yet easy enough for the novice.

Wash and dry the chicken well and with a very sharp knife make slits in the flesh of the breast, thighs and drumsticks to allow spices to penetrate.

In electric blender grind almonds, chironji or pastachios, poppy seeds, caraway and cummin. Combine these with the chilli powder, if used, and the ground coriander and turmeric. Pound saffron strands in mortar and pestle and dissolve in the boiling water, mix into yoghurt together with ground spices. Add 1½ teaspoons salt. Rub this marinade well into the chicken, inside and out, and let it marinate for at least 1 hour in the refrigerator. Put the hard boiled eggs into the cavity of the chicken and truss the bird, tucking its wing tips under and tying the drumsticks together.

In a large, heavy saucepan heat the ghee or oil and fry onion until golden brown. Remove onion from pan and reserve. Scrape excess marinade from outside of chicken, put chicken in pan and fry on all sides, taking care not to let it burn. Add the marinade, coriander, mint and chillies, the fried onion and hot water. Allow to come to simmering point, cover and simmer for 40 minutes. While chicken is cooking, wash rice well and soak in cold water for 30 minutes, then drain in colander.

Carefully lift chicken from pan. Measure stock in pan and make up to 4 cups with water if necessary. Return to pan, add remaining 2 teaspoons salt and the drained rice and bring to the boil, stirring to scrape any spice from base of pan. Put chicken on top of rice, sprinkle sultanas and peas around it, cover tightly and continue cooking for a further 30 minutes without lifting lid. Serve chicken surrounded by rice and garnished with silver leaf and fried nuts.

Murgh Jhal Frezi
Dry Fried Chicken   *Serves: 4–5*

1 x 1.5 kg (3 lb) roasting chicken
3 tablespoons ghee or oil
2 large onions, thinly sliced
1½ teaspoons chilli powder
½ cup water
½ cup yoghurt

Marinade:
1 teaspoon crushed garlic
1 teaspoon grated fresh ginger
1 teaspoon garam masala
 (page xxx)
1½ teaspoons salt
1 teaspoon ground coriander
1 teaspoon ground cummin
½ teaspoon ground turmeric
2 tablespoons yoghurt

Joint the chicken. Combine marinade ingredients and rub well over the chicken pieces. Set aside for 1 hour or longer.

Heat ghee or oil and fry the onions, stirring constantly, until they are evenly golden brown. Remove from the pan. In the same oil fry the chicken pieces until brown on both sides. Add the chilli powder, any remaining marinade and ½ cup water. Cover and simmer until tender. Stir yoghurt into gravy, return fried onions to pan and simmer 5 minutes longer.

Murgh Dum
Chicken in a Clay Pot (Bihar)   *Serves: 6*

1 x 1.5 kg (3 lb) roasting chicken
½ teaspoon crushed garlic
½ teaspoon finely grated fresh
  ginger
1 tablespoon grated onion
¼ teaspoon ground cardamom
¼ teaspoon ground turmeric
¼ teaspoon ground mace
1½ teaspoons salt
¼ teaspoon saffron strands or
  ⅛ teaspoon powdered saffron
1 tablespoon boiling water
3 tablespoons ghee or butter
⅓ cup strong chicken stock
1 bay leaf

Stuffing:
1 tablespoon ghee or oil
1 large onion, finely chopped
1 teaspoon finely chopped garlic
3 teaspoons ground coriander
1 teaspoon ground cummin
250 g (8 oz) minced lamb
½ teaspoon dried fenugreek
  leaves, optional
1 bay leaf
1½ teaspoons salt
½ teaspoon ground black
  pepper
¼ teaspoon each ground
  cardamom, cinnamon and
  cloves
1 cup long grain rice
2 cups hot water

If you own one of those clay casseroles it is ideal for cooking this dish in the oven, though any other heavy casserole may be used. In India the cooking is done over coals with more coals heaped on the lid of the pot. The spicing is very subtle, with no hot flavours at all, so this dish is a good introduction to Indian food.

Remove skin of chicken. You will find (if you have not done this before) that a skinned chicken is indeed a pathetic sight, but the reason for this procedure is that the flavours are not lost on the skin, but penetrate the flesh instead. However, without the protective skin which contains most of the fat, the breast meat is inclined to be dry, so remember to put the chicken breast downwards when cooking so that the breast is immersed in stock and remains moist.

Make small slashes in the flesh of the breast, thighs and drumsticks. Combine garlic, ginger, onion, cardamom, turmeric, mace and salt. Dissolve saffron in boiling water and add. Rub the mixture well into the chicken, cover and marinate overnight in refrigerator or for at least 2 hours at room temperature.

Fill the chicken with cooked and cooled stuffing, truss the bird and place in clay casserole breast downwards. Melt the ghee or butter and pour over the chicken. Pour stock into the casserole and add the bay leaf. Cover with lid, preferably sealing lid to base of casserole with a paste of flour and water so that none of the steam can escape. A little chapati dough (page 36) makes an excellent seal. This procedure is typical of dum cooking (steaming) so that none of the fragrant steam is lost.

Bake in a moderately slow oven 160°C (325°F) for 2 hours or a slow oven 150°C (300°F) for 4 hours if this is more convenient. Take the dish to the table and uncover it there, slipping a knife between pot and lid to break the seal. Serve with a pilau such as mattar pilau (page 21) or with plain boiled rice.

Stuffing: Heat ghee or oil and fry onion and garlic until soft and starting to turn golden. Add ground coriander and cummin and fry 1 minute, then add lamb and fry, stirring, until lamb is browned. Add all remaining ingredients except rice and water. Cover and cook on low heat for 15 minutes, stirring occasionally. Add rice and hot water, bring to the boil, stirring. Then turn heat very low, cover tightly and cook for 20–25 minutes or until liquid is absorbed by rice. Cool slightly before using.

Murgh Kaleja Kari

Curried Chicken Livers (North India)   *Serves: 4–5*

500 g (1 lb) chicken livers	½ teaspoon chilli powder
2 tablespoons ghee or oil	1 tablespoon ground coriander
2 medium onions, finely chopped	2 teaspoons ground cummin
1 teaspoon finely grated garlic	2 ripe tomatoes, peeled and chopped
2 teaspoons finely grated fresh ginger	1 teaspoon salt
½ teaspoon ground turmeric	1 teaspoon garam masala (page xxx)

Wash the livers and drain in a colander. Cut them in halves and if there are any yellow spots on the livers slice them off with a sharp knife.

Heat the ghee or oil in a heavy saucepan and fry the onion, stirring occasionally, until soft. Add the garlic and ginger and continue frying until golden. Add turmeric, chilli powder, coriander and cummin. Fry for 2 minutes, stirring, then add the tomatoes and salt and cook, covered, on low heat until tomatoes are puréed, stirring occasionally. Add the chicken livers and stir gently. Replace lid and cook for 15 minutes, sprinkle garam masala over and simmer for 1–2 minutes. Serve hot with rice and other accompaniments.

Murgh Kari
Madras Chicken Curry (South India)   *Serves: 6*

1 x 1.5 kg (3 lb) roasting chicken
3 tablespoons oil
12 curry leaves
2 medium onions, finely chopped
2 teaspoons finely chopped
   fresh ginger
1 teaspoon ground turmeric

3 teaspoons chilli powder
3 teaspoons ground coriander
1 teaspoon ground cummin
1 large, ripe tomato, peeled and
   chopped
2 small sticks cinnamon
2 cups coconut milk (page xxxv)

This curry is delicious, but certainly hot because of the amount of chilli used. If you like hot curries, this is for you but if not simply cut down or omit the chilli powder and it will still be a flavoursome dish with plenty of rich coconut milk gravy.

Cut chicken into curry pieces (page 89). Heat oil, fry curry leaves, onions, garlic and ginger until soft. Add turmeric, chilli powder, coriander, cummin and fry for 2 minutes. Add salt and tomato, stir well, cover and cook until tomato is pulpy. Add chicken and cinnamon sticks and stir well until chicken is coated with the spice mixture. Cover and cook for 30 minutes, or until chicken is almost tender. Stir in the coconut milk and simmer, uncovered, for about 15 minutes longer. Serve with rice and accompaniments.

Murgh Mattar Kari
Curried Chicken with Fresh Peas (Punjab)   *Serves: 6*

1 x 1.5 kg (3 lb) roasting chicken
2 large onions
2 teaspoons chopped garlic
2 fresh red chillies, seeded and
   chopped
2 tablespoons desiccated
   coconut
2 tablespoons water

3 tablespoons ghee or oil
1 teaspoon garam masala
   (page xxx)
2 teaspoons salt
1 cup water
¾ cup shelled fresh peas
2 tablespoons chopped fresh
   coriander or mint
2 tablespoons lemon juice

Cut chicken into curry pieces (page 89). Finely slice one onion and set aside. Roughly chop the other onion and put into electric blender with the garlic, ginger, chillies and coconut. Add about 2 tablespoons water to facilitate blending and blend to a smooth paste.

Heat 2 tablespoons ghee or oil in a heavy saucepan and fry the sliced onion, stirring, until it is golden brown. Remove from pan. Add remaining tablespoon ghee to the pan and fry the blended mixture until brown, stirring constantly. When ghee or oil shows around edges add the ground cummin and garam masala and fry for a few seconds more. Add the chicken pieces and turn them in the spice mixture, then add salt, water and shelled peas. Cook, covered, until peas and chicken are almost tender. Add fried onions and cook 10 minutes longer. Remove from heat, stir in fresh coriander and lemon juice and serve with rice or chapatis.

Khobani Murgh
Chicken with Apricots (Kashmir)   *Serves: 4–5*

1 x 1.5 kg (3 lb) roasting chicken
2 tablespoons ghee or oil
3 fresh green chillies, seeded and chopped
1 teaspoon finely grated fresh ginger
1 teaspoon finely chopped garlic
3 medium onions, finely sliced

2 cardamom pods, bruised
1 small stick cinnamon
1 large ripe tomato, chopped
2 teaspoons salt
½ cup hot water
⅛ teaspoon saffron strands
1 tablespoon boiling milk or water
1 cup dried apricot halves

Kashmiri dried apricots are very different from those we get here – the whole fruit is dried, and it is very hard and needs soaking overnight. However, dried apricot or nectarine halves may be substituted, but do not need soaking.

Cut the chicken into joints. Heat ghee or oil in a large, heavy saucepan and fry the chillies, ginger, garlic, onions, cardamom and cinnamon until onion is golden. Add chicken pieces and fry, turning them in the mixture. Add tomato, salt and hot water. Cover and simmer 30 minutes.

Meanwhile, crush saffron strands in mortar and pestle and dissolve in boiling milk or water. Add saffron and apricots to the pan, stir, replace lid and continue simmering for a further 10 minutes or until chicken is cooked. Apricots should be tender but not mushy. Serve with pilau rice (page 18).

Murgh Masala
Roast Chicken with Spicy Stuffing (Hyderabad)   *Serves: 4–5*

1 x 1.5 kg (3 lb) roasting chicken
1½ teaspoons salt
½ teaspoon ground black
   pepper
½ teaspoon ground turmeric
½ teaspoon crushed garlic
½ teaspoon finely grated fresh
   ginger
1 teaspoon ghee
1½ cups hot water
8 small new potatoes

Stuffing:
2 tablespoons ghee or oil
1 medium onion, finely
   chopped
3 teaspoons garlic, finely
   chopped
½ teaspoon finely grated fresh
   ginger
2 fresh red or green chillies,
   seeded and chopped
1 teaspoon ground coriander
1 teaspoon chilli powder
1 teaspoon garam masala
   (page xxx)
250 g (8 oz) minced lamb
1 ripe tomato, chopped
½ teaspoon salt
1 or 2 tablespoons raisins
1 tablespoon vinegar or
   lemon juice
2 tablespoons yoghurt
2 hard boiled eggs, chopped
20 blanched almonds
2 tablespoons chopped fresh
   coriander

Gravy:
1 teaspoon cummin
1 tablespoon ghee or oil
1 medium onion, finely chopped
1 fresh red or green chilli, seeded
   and chopped
1 teaspoon garlic, crushed
½ teaspoon finely grated fresh
   ginger
½ teaspoon chilli powder
2 ripe tomatoes, peeled and
   chopped
2 teaspoons white poppy seeds
   or ground almonds
½ teaspoon garam masala
   (page xxx)
stock from chicken
2 tablespoons chopped fresh
   coriander

Wash and dry the chicken inside and out, and rub well all over with salt, pepper, turmeric, garlic and ginger. Allow to marinate while preparing the stuffing.

Fill chicken with stuffing, close body opening and tie drumsticks together with string. Place in a roasting pan with ghee and hot water. Place potatoes, scrubbed but not peeled, around chicken. Roast in a moderate oven, 180°C (350°F), basting every 20 minutes or so, for about 1¼ hours or until chicken is cooked.

While chicken is roasting prepare gravy up to the point where the stock from the pan has to be added, then quickly finish the gravy and serve with the chicken.

Stuffing: Heat ghee or oil and fry onion, garlic, ginger and chillies over gentle heat until they are soft and start to turn golden. Add spices and stir for a few seconds, then add minced lamb and stir over medium heat until meat is browned. Add tomato, salt, raisins, vinegar or lemon juice and yoghurt, cover and simmer for 10 minutes. Remove from heat and stir in the eggs, almonds and coriander.

Gravy: Roast cummin seeds in a dry pan over medium heat stirring constantly until the colour changes and a pleasant aroma is given off. Grind with pestle and mortar. Heat ghee or oil and fry onion, chilli, garlic and ginger until brown. Add chilli powder, tomatoes, poppy seeds, cummin, garam masala and cook gently until tomatoes have softened and may be pulped by stirring with a spoon. Add the chicken stock from the roasting pan, making it up to ¾ cup with hot water if necessary, and spooning off any excess fat. Bring back to the boil, taste and adjust seasoning if required. Stir in coriander leaves and pour into a separate bowl to accompany the chicken.

Badhak Vindaloo
Duck Vindaloo (Goa)   *Serves: 4–5*

1 x 2.5 kg (5 lb) duck
10 dried red chillies, preferably
    Kashmiri or Goan chillies
¾ cup vinegar
1 tablespoon chopped garlic
1 tablespoon chopped fresh
    ginger
1 tablespoon ground coriander

2 teaspoons ground cummin
1 teaspoon ground turmeric
½ teaspoon ground black
    pepper
2–3 tablespoons ghee or oil
2 teaspoons salt
1 tablespoon sugar

Cut the duck into joints. Remove stalks and seeds from dried chillies and soak in vinegar for about 10 minutes. Put chillies, vinegar, garlic and ginger into electric blender and blend until smooth. Scrape mixture out of blender into a large bowl and mix in the ground spices. Add pieces of duck, turn them over in the mixture until they are well coated, cover and leave for 2 hours at room temperature or overnight in the refrigerator.

In a large saucepan heat the ghee or oil and fry the pieces of duck lightly. Add salt and a little hot water together with any marinade left. Cover and simmer on low heat until duck is tender, adding a little more water if necessary during cooking. At end of cooking time stir in the sugar. Serve with rice.

Note: As vindaloos have a high acid content, it is preferable to cook them in an enamel or stainless steel pan.

Kanda Papeta Ma Batak
Duck with Potatoes and Onions (Maharashtra Parsi)   *Serves: 4–5*

1 x 2 kg (4 lb) roasting duck
1 teaspoon crushed garlic
1 teaspoon finely grated ginger
1 teaspoon ground turmeric
1 teaspoon ground black pepper
3 tablespoons oil
12–15 small pickling onions,
    peeled and left whole
12 small new potatoes, scrubbed
2 large onions, finely chopped

2 teaspoons chilli powder
3 fresh green chillies, slit and
    seeded
2 small sticks cinnamon
8 whole cloves
8 cardamom pods, bruised
2½ teaspoons salt
½ cup vinegar
3 cups water
1 tablespoon sugar

Joint the duck and rub all over with the garlic, ginger, turmeric and black pepper mixed together. Leave aside for 1 hour. Heat the oil in a large saucepan and brown the whole onions and potatoes lightly. Remove from pan and set aside. Put in the chopped onion and fry, stirring, until soft and golden. Add the chilli powder and stir for a few seconds, then add the pieces of duck and brown them. Add the green chillies, whole spices, salt, vinegar and water, cover and simmer gently for 2 hours or until duck is almost tender, adding extra hot water if necessary. Put in potatoes and onions for the last 30 minutes of cooking time. Stir in sugar at the end and serve with plain or pilau rice (page 18).

Parsi Poro

Parsi Omelette (Maharashtra Parsi)   *Serves: 2*

1 cup diced potato	2 tablespoons finely chopped
2 tablespoons ghee or oil	fresh coriander
4 eggs	1 small onion, finely chopped
¾ teaspoon salt	2 fresh red or green chillies,
¼ teaspoon pepper	seeded and chopped
½ teaspoon ground cummin	

Parboil potato in lightly salted boiling water for a minute or two, drain well in colander.

Heat ghee or oil in a frying pan and fry the potato until lightly browned. Lift out on slotted spoon and set aside. Separate eggs and beat the whites until frothy, then beat in the yolks, salt, pepper and cummin. Fold in coriander, onion and chillies. Heat omelette pan or clean frying pan with ghee left from frying potatoes, and if necessary add a little extra ghee. Pour in the egg mixture and when it starts to set add the fried potato, distributing it evenly over the omelette. Cook on low heat until golden brown on bottom, turn omelette over and cook until brown on other side. Serve hot with chapatis or bread.

Akoori
Parsi Scrambled Eggs (Maharashtra Parsi)   *Serves: 4–6*

6–8 eggs
4 tablespoons milk
3/4 teaspoon salt
1/4 teaspoon ground black
  pepper
2 tablespoons ghee or butter
6 spring onions or 2 small white
  onions, finely chopped
2–3 fresh red or green chillies,
  seeded and chopped

1 teaspoon finely grated fresh
  ginger
1/8 teaspoon ground turmeric
2 tablespoons chopped fresh
  coriander leaves
1 ripe tomato, peeled and diced,
  optional
1/2 teaspoon ground cummin

Garnish:
tomato wedges
sprig of fresh coriander leaves

*Among India's many races and religions, it is the Parsi community
that makes the most use of eggs, and a touch of Parsi genius with
scrambled eggs turns a simple dish into a feast. No book on Indian
cooking would be complete without this favourite recipe.*

Beat eggs until well mixed. Add the milk, salt and pepper. Heat ghee
or butter in a large, heavy frying pan and cook the onions, chillies
and ginger until soft. Add turmeric, coriander leaves and tomato, if
used, and fry for a minute or two longer, then stir in the egg mixture
and the ground cummin. Cook over low heat, stirring and lifting the
eggs as they begin to set on the base of the pan. Mix and cook until
the eggs are of a creamy consistency – they should not be cooked
until dry. Turn on to a serving plate and garnish with tomato and
coriander. Serve with chapatis, parathas or toasted bread.

Bhaji per Eenda
Eggs on Spinach (Maharashtra Parsi)   *Serves: 4*

1 bunch spinach
1 tablespoon ghee or butter
1 small onion, finely chopped
1 teaspoon finely chopped
  garlic
1 teaspoon finely grated ginger

1/2 teaspoon cummin seeds
1/8 teaspoon chilli powder,
  optional
salt and ground black pepper
  to taste
6 eggs

Wash the spinach very thoroughly, discard any tough stems and cook the leaves in very little water in a covered pan for 10–12 minutes or until soft. Drain and chop the spinach.

In a frying pan heat the ghee or butter and fry the onion, garlic, ginger and cummin until onion is soft and turning golden. Mix in the chopped spinach. Add the chilli powder (if used) and salt and pepper to taste.

Beat the eggs in a bowl and season to taste with salt and pepper. Pour over the spinach mixture in the pan, cover pan and cook on low heat until eggs set. Serve hot.

Mootay Molee
Egg and Coconut Curry (Kerala)   *Serves: 4–6*

6–8 eggs	6 curry leaves
2 tablespoons oil	1 teaspoon ground turmeric
1 medium onion, finely sliced	2 cups thin coconut milk
1½ teaspoons crushed garlic	(page xxxv)
1 teaspoon finely grated fresh ginger	1½ cups thick coconut milk (page xxxv)
2 or 3 fresh green chillies, seeded and sliced	1 teaspoon salt
	lemon juice to taste

Put the eggs into cold water, bring slowly to the boil, stirring for the first 5 minutes to centre the yolks. Simmer for 10 minutes, then cool quickly under running cold water. Shell the eggs and set aside.

Heat oil in a saucepan and fry the onion, garlic, ginger, chillies and curry leaves on a low heat until onions are soft without letting them brown. Add turmeric and stir, then add the thin coconut milk and simmer uncovered for 10 minutes. Add the thick coconut milk and salt and stir constantly while letting it come to simmering point. Cut the eggs in halves lengthways and simmer them in the coconut gravy for a few minutes, just until heated through. Remove from heat, stir in lemon juice to taste. Serve with white rice.

Keema per Eenda
Eggs with Savoury Mince (Maharashtra Parsi)   *Serves: 4*

2 tablespoons ghee or oil
1 large onion, finely chopped
2 fresh green chillies, seeded
  and chopped
2 teaspoons finely chopped
  ginger
2 teaspoons ground coriander
1 teaspoon ground cummin
1 teaspoon chilli powder,
  optional
1 teaspoon ground turmeric

750 g (1½ lb) minced lamb or
  beef
1 ripe tomato, peeled and
  chopped
1½ teaspoons salt
½ cup water
pinch of sugar, optional
1 tablespoon garam masala
1 teaspoon finely chopped fresh
  coriander
4 eggs
salt and ground black pepper
  to taste

Heat ghee or oil and fry the onion, chillies, garlic and ginger until golden. Add ground spices, stir and fry for 1 minute, then add the meat and fry, stirring until it changes colour. Add tomato, salt and ½ cup water. Some cooks like to add a pinch of sugar. Cover and cook until meat is tender and liquid almost all absorbed. Sprinkle in the garam masala and half the fresh coriander and mix. Spread meat in a buttered ovenproof dish, make 4 depressions with the back of a spoon and break an egg into each one. Season eggs with pepper and salt.

Bake in a moderately hot oven 190°C (375°F) until the eggs are set. Sprinkle with remaining fresh coriander and serve immediately, with parathas or naan.

Note: A variation on this dish is to beat the egg whites stiffly, mix in the yolks and season with salt and pepper, then to spread this mixture over the meat and bake until the eggs are set.

Meats

It is in the north of India, in the areas influenced by the Moghuls, that most meat is eaten. It is always lamb or mutton and is superbly presented, whether in combination with rice in a rich biriani or in a spiced dish to be eaten with the flat wheaten breads.

I was in Kashmir on the Moslem festival of *Id-uz-Zaha* or *Bakri Id*. This festival commemorates Ibrahim's (Abraham's) willingness to sacrifice his son Ishak (Isaac) and how he was spared when God provided an animal to take his place on the sacrificial altar. On this day Moslems go to the mosques early in the day and return to their homes to carry out the ritual slaughter.

Behind the houseboat on which we were staying the men of the family who owned the boat killed a number of sheep according to ritual and distributed the meat to relations and friends and to the poor, which is the custom.

It was also in Kashmir that we partook of a *waswan* – a festive meal served on an auspicious occasion or to mark a celebration. A *trami* or round tray is served to each group of four diners, and is traditionally placed on a white cloth spread on a rug. Diners sit on the floor and eat with the fingers. Before eating, hands are washed by pouring water from a *tashtanari*, which is part of the ceremony.

When presented, the *trami* contains rice and a few different mutton preparations and is topped by *seekh kebab*. It is covered with a high domed lid, the *surpush*, and on top of this is a plate of raw vegetables – tomatoes, onions, fresh limes, which is served as a relish.

The original *waswan*, I was told, featured 35 different dishes, many of which are based on meat. As diners eat those dishes which were first served, the cook brings around fresh offerings in the pots in which they are cooked, and ladles a new dish onto each diner's portion. Although each dish was truly delicious, it was with relief that I found this *waswan* only comprised a dozen or so different items.

Among them were *tabak maaz*, tender lamb or goat ribs fried with spices; *methi maaz*, chopped mutton cooked with fresh fenugreek which is particularly delicious; *rista*, meatballs made from lamb which has been pounded to velvety smoothness, lightly spiced, and cooked with saffron; various fresh chutneys and vegetable dishes; and the *waswan* always ends with the most important dish, *gushtaba* (meatballs in a creamy yoghurt sauce).

Firni is offered for dessert (creamy, rose-flavoured rice custard) and *qahwah* (Kashmiri spiced tea served in a samovar) ends the feast.

Most of the meat eaten in India is mutton, which can mean lamb or goat. Beef is eaten by certain communities, but it comes from buffaloes rather than cattle as the cow is sacred to the Hindus.

While Moslems are great meat eaters (they believe health and strength comes from eating meat as often as possible), pork is forbidden them and indeed they have such an aversion to it that it is not just a religious taboo – they will not touch it under any circumstances. Among the Christians in Goa and other parts of South India, however, pork is popular and they have a number of festive dishes based on pork – dishes such as *sorpotel*.

I have found that cheaper cuts of meat take better to the dishes of India, since the spices used in curries, *kormas* and other meat dishes develop wonderful flavour while the meat cooks to tenderness. So have no qualms about using mutton in preference to the more expensive and tender lamb. Use only the best lamb, however, in dishes such as *kebabs* where the meat is grilled for only a few minutes.

In the recipes in this book I have used mostly lamb or mutton, but use beef in any of the recipes if this meat is preferred. Here again, choose cuts that will stand up to long, slow cooking but always trim off any fat or connective tissue very carefully.

Rista
Mutton Koftas in Saffron Sauce (Kashmir)   *Serves: 6*

1 kg (2 lb) boneless lamb
½ teaspoon ground cardamom
1 teaspoon garam masala
    (page xxx)
2 teaspoons salt
3 tablespoons arrowroot
2 tablespoons cold water
1 teaspoon ground turmeric
3 teaspoons chilli powder,
    or to taste
2 tablespoons ghee
2 tablespoons oil

125 g (4 oz) finely sliced shallots
    or brown onions
2 teaspoons finely chopped
    fresh ginger
4 whole brown cardamoms or
    small green cardamoms,
    bruised
4 whole cloves
1 small stick cinnamon
2 teaspoons paprika
2 teaspoons tomato paste
¼ teaspoon saffron strands
2 tablespoons boiling water

Cut the meat into 2.5 cm (1 inch) cubes and divide into four portions. Process one portion at a time in food processor, using steel chopping blade, until it is a smooth, thick paste. Mix in the ground cardamom, garam masala and salt and the arrowroot mixed smoothly with the cold water. Form into large balls and parboil in lightly salted water for 10 minutes, adding half the turmeric and chilli powder to the water.

Heat ghee and oil, fry the onions and whole spices. Add remaining turmeric, chilli powder and paprika and tomato paste. Add the meatballs and the stock in which they were cooked. Cover and simmer until tender. Dissolve saffron in the boiling water and add towards end of cooking. Serve hot with plain white rice.

Mutton Sula

Barbecued Spiced Mutton (Rajasthan)   *Serves: 4*

500 g (1 lb) boneless lamb
1 teaspoon ajowan seeds
1 teaspoon chilli powder
1 teaspoon ground turmeric
2 teaspoons ground coriander
pinch of ground cloves
1 teaspoon crushed garlic
1 teaspoon salt
1 teaspoon finely grated fresh
    ginger
1 cup yoghurt

Garnish:
lemon slices
1 medium onion, finely sliced

Cut lamb into small cubes. Crush the ajowan seeds and combine with the other spices. Crush garlic with salt. Mix spices, salt, garlic and ginger with the yoghurt, pour over the lamb and mix well. Marinate the lamb in this mixture for at least 5 hours.

Thread the pieces of meat on skewers and grill over charcoal fire or under preheated grill, turning the skewers frequently, until the meat is well done.

Push the meat off the skewers onto the serving plate, garnish with lemon slices and finely sliced onions. This is usually served with naan (page 38), podina chatni (page 139) and pickles.

Gushtaba
Mutton Koftas in Yoghurt Sauce (Kashmir)   *Serves: 6*

1 kg (2 lb) lean, boneless lamb
1 teaspoon Kashmiri garam
   masala (page xxx)
2 teaspoons salt
4 tablespoons arrowroot
3 tablespoons cold water
2 tablespoons ghee
2 tablespoons oil
2 teaspoons finely chopped
   fresh ginger
1 cup finely sliced shallots or
   brown onions
2 tablespoons besan (chick pea
   flour)
2 cups yoghurt
1 small stick cinnamon
4 whole cloves
3 whole brown cardamoms
   or whole green cardamoms,
   bruised

Garnish:
2 tablespoons finely chopped
   mint or coriander

Cut the meat into 2.5 cm (1 inch) cubes. Divide into four portions and use chopping blade in food processor to convert one portion at a time to a thick, smooth paste. Mix in the Kashmiri garam masala, salt and arrowroot mixed to a smooth cream with the cold water. Knead well until evenly combined, then form into large balls about the size of an egg. Bring a saucepan of lightly salted water to the boil and cook the meatballs for 10 minutes.

In another pan heat ghee and oil and slowly cook the ginger and shallots or brown onions until golden. Remove pan from heat, sift in the besan. Return to heat and cook, stirring, for two minutes. Beat yoghurt until smooth and add to the pan. Stir constantly until the oil separates from the mass. Add the meatballs and enough of the stock in which they cooked to almost cover them. Add whole spices. Simmer 30–40 minutes or until very tender. Stir frequently and keep heat low to prevent sauce curdling. If liquid evaporates add a little more stock. There should be a generous amount of creamy sauce.

Serve the gushtaba sprinkled with chopped fresh mint or coriander and accompanied by plain white rice and other accompaniments.

Mutton Doh Piaza

Curried Mutton with Onions (Uttar Pradesh)   *Serves: 8–10*

1.5 kg (3 lb) shoulder or leg of lamb
1 kg (2 lb) onions
4 teaspoons chopped garlic
2 teaspoons chopped fresh ginger
3 tablespoons yoghurt
2 teaspoons chilli powder, or to taste
1 teaspoon paprika

3 tablespoons chopped fresh coriander
2 tablespoons ground coriander
2 teaspoons black cummin seeds
3 tablespoons ghee
3 tablespoons oil
8 cardamom pods, bruised
1 teaspoon garam masala (page xxx)

Cut meat into large cubes. Slice half the onions finely and roughly chop the rest. Put chopped onions into electric blender with garlic, ginger, yoghurt, chilli powder, paprika, fresh coriander, ground coriander and black cummin seeds. Blend until smooth.

Heat ghee and oil in a large heavy pan and fry the sliced onions, stirring frequently, until evenly browned. Remove from pan. Add cubed meat to pan, not too many pieces at once, and fry on high heat until browned on all sides. Remove each batch as it is browned and add more. When all the meat has been done and removed from pan, add a little more ghee or oil if necessary and fry the blended mixture over medium heat, stirring all the time, until it is cooked and gives out an aromatic smell. Oil should start to appear around the edges of mixture. Return meat to pan, add cardamom pods, stir well, cover and cook on low heat until meat is almost tender. Stir occasionally. It may be necessary to add a little water, but usually the juices given out by the meat are sufficient to complete the cooking. When meat is tender and liquid almost absorbed add garam masala and reserved fried onions, replace lid of pan and leave on very low heat for a further 15 minutes. Serve with rice or Indian breads.

Mutton Korma
Braised Mutton with Yoghurt (North India)   *Serves: 4–6*

750 g (1½ lb) lean lamb
2 large onions
3 teaspoons chopped fresh
   ginger
2 teaspoons chopped garlic
2 tablespoons blanched
   almonds
2 dried red chillies, preferably
   Kashmiri chillies
¾ cup water
2 teaspoons white poppy seeds,
   ground
2 teaspoons ground coriander

1 teaspoon ground cummin
1 teaspoon garam masala
   (page xxx)
¼ teaspoon saffron strands
2 tablespoons boiling water
½ cup yoghurt
1½ teaspoons salt
2 tablespoons ghee or oil
2 tablespoons chopped fresh
   coriander

*A rich, thick gravy clings around the pieces of meat, making this ideal
to serve with Indian breads. Spicy but not hot.*

Trim off excess fat and cut meat into large cubes. Peel and roughly
chop one onion and put into electric blender with ginger, garlic,
almonds and the dried chillies. For a mild result discard seeds of
chillies. Add ½ cup water and blend on high speed until ingredients
are smoothly ground. Add poppy seeds and the ground spices and
blend for a couple of seconds longer.

Pound saffron strands in mortar and pestle, then dissolve in the
boiling water. Mix with the yoghurt and salt and set aside.

Heat ghee or oil and fry the remaining onion, finely sliced, until
golden. Add the blended mixture and fry, stirring with a wooden
spoon, until it smells fragrant and looks oily. Rinse out blender
container with ¼ cup water and add to pan, then stir until liquid
dries up again. Add the meat and stir until each piece is coated with
the spice. Add the saffron and yoghurt mixture, stir well, cover and
cook on low heat for 1 hour or until meat is tender and all the juices
given out by the meat have been reabsorbed, leaving the gravy very
thick. Stir occasionally towards end of cooking to ensure gravy does
not stick to base of pan. Add coriander during last 5 minutes of
cooking.

Serve hot, accompanied by chapatis or parathas or plain white
rice.

Mutton Bohlapuri
Mutton Curry (Maharashtra)   *Serves: 6–8*

1 kg (2 lb) lean mutton
6 green chillies, seeded and
    roughly chopped
3 tablespoons chopped fresh
    coriander
3 teaspoons chopped garlic
1 tablespoon chopped fresh
    ginger
1 teaspoon ground turmeric
4 tablespoons ghee or oil
4 medium onions, finely
    chopped
1 cup water
2 teaspoons salt
2 tablespoons desiccated
    coconut

1 teaspoon fennel seeds
1 teaspoon white poppy seeds,
    optional
1 tablespoon ground coriander
1 tablespoon ground cummin
¼ teaspoon grated nutmeg
250 g (8 oz) tomatoes, peeled
    and chopped
250 g (8 oz) potatoes, peeled and
    cubed
1 cup coconut milk (page xxxv)

Garnish:
1 large onion
pakorha batter (page 48)
oil for deep frying

Trim off any fat and cut mutton into cubes. Grind chillies, coriander, garlic, ginger and turmeric to a paste in electric blender, adding as little water as necessary to facilitate blending. Marinate the meat in this mixture for 2 hours or longer.

Heat ghee or oil in a large, heavy saucepan and fry the onions, stirring, until golden brown. Add meat and fry on high heat until browned. Add water and salt and simmer, covered, until meat is tender, about 30 minutes. Meanwhile roast the coconut, fennel seeds and white poppy seeds (if used) separately in a dry pan until golden brown, stirring constantly. Grind very fine in blender or pound with mortar and pestle. Add to pan together with the coriander, cummin, nutmeg, tomatoes. Stir well, cover and cook for 20 minutes. Add the potatoes and a little water if necessary, continue cooking for a further 20 minutes or until potatoes are cooked. Stir in coconut milk and cook uncovered for a further 10 minutes. Serve hot, garnished with onion ring pakorhas and accompanied by rice or puris.

Garnish: Cut onion into fairly thick slices and separate into rings. Dip in pakorha batter (page 48) and deep fry in hot oil. Drain on absorbent paper.

Roghan Josh
Kashmiri Lamb Curry   *Serves 4–6*

750 g (1½ lb) lean lamb
3 dried red chillies, seeded
½ cup hot water
3 teaspoons chopped garlic
1 tablespoon chopped fresh
  ginger
2 tablespoons desiccated
  coconut, toasted
2 tablespoons blanched
  almonds
1 teaspoon ground cummin
1 teaspoon poppy seeds
½ teaspoon ground fennel
½ teaspoon ground cardamom
¼ teaspoon ground cloves
¼ teaspoon ground mace

½ teaspoon ground black
  pepper
¼ teaspoon saffron strands
2 tablespoons boiling water
4 tablespoons ghee or oil
1 medium onion, finely chopped
4 cardamom pods, bruised
½ teaspoon ground turmeric
½ cup yoghurt
2 ripe tomatoes, peeled and
  chopped
1½ teaspoons salt
1 teaspoon Kashmiri garam
  masala (page xxx)
2 tablespoons chopped fresh
  coriander

Cut the lamb into large cubes. Soak chillies in the hot water for 5 minutes. Put garlic, ginger, coconut (shake in a dry pan over medium heat to toast), almonds and chillies together with 2 tablespoons of the soaking water into electric blender. Put ground coriander, cummin, poppy seeds and fennel in a small pan and shake over low heat for a few minutes until spices darken slightly in colour and give off an aromatic smell. Add to the ingredients in blender. Blend for a few seconds until smooth. Remove from blender container and add the ground cardamom, cloves, mace and pepper. Pound saffron, dissolve in boiling water and add to spices. Set aside.

Heat ghee or oil in a large heavy saucepan and fry the chopped onion, stirring, until onion is golden brown. Add bruised cardamoms, turmeric and the blended spice mixture and fry, stirring, until well cooked and the ghee starts to separate from the spices. Add the yoghurt, a spoonful at a time and stir it in. Add tomatoes and salt, stir and fry for a further 5 minutes, then add the cubed lamb and cook over high heat, stirring and turning meat so that each piece is coated with the spice. Turn heat very low, cover and cook for 1 hour or longer. Lamb should be very tender and liquid almost absorbed. Stir occasionally to ensure that spices don't stick to base of pan. Sprinkle with garam masala, replace lid and cook 5 minutes longer. Serve sprinkled with coriander leaves and accompanied by plain rice or a pilau.

Pasanda
Spiced Lamb Slices (Kashmir)   *Serves: 4*

500 g (1 lb) lean lamb from
    leg
3 teaspoons chopped garlic
2 teaspoons chopped fresh
    ginger
1/8 teaspoon ground cloves
1 medium onion, chopped
1 teaspoon fennel seeds
1 teaspoon salt
small pinch asafoetida,
    optional

1/2 cup yoghurt
1 teaspoon chilli powder
2 teaspoons ground coriander
2 tablespoons ghee
2 tablespoons oil
1/4 teaspoon saffron strands
1 tablespoon boiling water
2 or 3 drops kewra essence
1/2 cup hot water
1/2 cup finely chopped fresh
    coriander

Trim all fat from the meat and cut meat into thin slices like small schnitzels. Beat with a meat mallet to flatten. These are pasandas.

In electric blender grind the garlic, ginger, cloves, onion and fennel seeds, salt and asafoetida until smooth. Mix with the yoghurt, chilli powder, coriander and rub over the pasandas. Marinate for at least 2 hours.

Heat ghee and oil in a heavy frying pan and fry the pieces of meat over fairly high heat, turning them frequently. Pound saffron strands in mortar and pestle and dissolve in a tablespoon of boiling water, then mix in the kewra flavouring. Set aside. Add about 1/4 cup hot water to pan, cover and cook until the liquid evaporates. Stir to release meat and spice marinade from base of pan. Add another 1/4 cup water and repeat. When this has evaporated, sprinkle over the saffron and kewra liquid, cover and leave for a few minutes, then serve the pasandas sprinkled with fresh coriander. If liked, fried potatoes may be added to the meat and stirred through just before turning off the heat.

Serve with a salad of onions, tomatoes and chillies such as kachumbar (page 135).

Shami Kebab
Minced Lamb and Lentil Patties
(Uttar Pradesh)

*Makes 8 large or
24 cocktail size patties*

750 g (1½ lb) finely minced lamb
1 medium onion, finely
   chopped
3 tablespoons yellow split peas
   (mattar dahl — page 62) or red
   lentils (masoor dhal)
1 teaspoon finely grated fresh
   ginger
1½ teaspoon finely chopped
   garlic
1½ teaspoons salt
2 cups water
½ teaspoon garam masala
   (page xxx)
1 tablespoon yoghurt or thick
   cream
1 small egg, beaten
ghee or oil for shallow frying

Filling:
1 fresh green chilli, seeded and
   chopped
1 tablespoon finely chopped
   fresh coriander
1 spring onion, including green
   leaves
½ teaspoon finely grated fresh
   ginger

Put lamb, onion, dhal, ginger, garlic, salt and water into a heavy saucepan and bring to the boil, stirring. Cover and cook over low heat until meat, lentils and onions are soft, about 45 minutes. Then uncover and cook, stirring now and then, until all the liquid has been absorbed. This may take at least 1 hour. Leave to cool, then mix in the garam masala and yoghurt or cream. Add 1 tablespoon of beaten egg and mix well. If mixture is not too moist add more of the beaten egg. Knead very well for 10 minutes or until mixture is completely smooth.

Divide into 8 portions and form each into a flat circle. Put ½ teaspoonful of filling in the middle, close the meat mixture around it, pinching edges together. Flatten gently to form a small round patty. Shallow fry on a heavy griddle or frying pan lightly greased with ghee or oil. Serve hot. If serving these as cocktail snacks and making them bite-size, it is easier not to use a filling but to serve with podina chatni (page 139) for dipping.

Filling: Chop spring onion very finely. Mix all the ingredients together.

Sali Jardaloo Boti
Lamb and Apricots with Potato Straws
(Maharashtra Parsi)   *Serves: 6*

250 g (8 oz) dried apricots
1.5 kg (3 lb) lean lamb or mutton
10 dried red chillies, seeds removed
1 tablespoon chopped fresh ginger
1 tablespoon chopped garlic
2 teaspoons ground cummin
3 tablespoons ghee or oil
2 large onions, finely chopped
1 teaspoon ground cinnamon
½ teaspoon ground cloves
½ teaspoon ground black pepper

½ teaspoon ground cardamom
500 g (1 lb) ripe tomatoes peeled, seeded and chopped
2½ teaspoons salt
1 tablespoon jaggery or brown sugar
2 tablespoons malt vinegar

Garnish:
2 tablespoons chopped fresh coriander
1 cup potato straws

In India, this dish is prepared using Kashmiri apricots which are dried whole, complete with seed. The recipe was given to me by ladies who are acknowledged good cooks of the Parsi community. When I cooked it I had to substitute dried apricot halves, which are different to those I tasted in Bombay but rather good. This is not a very spicy dish though it does include some of the curry spices.

Soak apricots in water 30 minutes, drain. Cut meat into small cubes, discarding any fat. Soak chillies in hot water for 10 minutes. In electric blender grind ginger, garlic, cummin and chillies to a paste, adding a little water to facilitate blending. Marinate the meat in half this paste for 1 hour.

Heat ghee or oil in heavy saucepan and fry the onion until golden brown. Add remaining ground paste and the dry ground spices and stir well. Add meat and fry until browned, then add the tomatoes and salt, cover and cook on low heat until meat is tender, adding a little water if necessary. Lastly add jaggery or sugar and vinegar and the apricots and simmer on very low heat for 15 minutes. Serve garnished with chopped coriander and potato straws.

Mutton Sohitya
Curried Lamb with Sweet Corn (Rajasthan)   *Serves: 4*

500 g (1 lb) lamb shoulder or
    forequarter
4 tablespoons oil or ghee
4 medium onions, finely sliced
1 stick cinnamon
4 whole cloves
6 black peppercorns
2 bay leaves
1 teaspoon finely chopped fresh
    ginger
1 teaspoon finely chopped garlic
1 tablespoon ground coriander
2 large ripe tomatoes, peeled
    and chopped
1 cup corn kernels
1½ teaspoons salt
1 cup yoghurt
squeeze of lemon juice
2 tablespoons chopped fresh
    coriander

Garnish:
few sprigs fresh coriander
1 onion, finely sliced
tomato roses
cherry tomatoes

Cut lamb into cubes, and reserve any bones to cook with the meat as this gives the dish good flavour.

Heat the oil or ghee in a large, heavy saucepan and fry the onions with cinnamon, cloves, peppercorns and bay leaves. Stir occasionally and when onions are golden add the ginger and garlic and continue stirring until these too turn golden brown. Stir in the ground coriander, then the tomatoes, corn and salt. Cover and cook for 5 minutes, then add the lamb and bring to the boil. Cook for 10 minutes before stirring in the yoghurt, beaten until smooth. Cover and simmer until meat is tender, adding a little hot water if necessary. Just before serving add lemon juice and chopped coriander. Garnish the curry with extra coriander leaves, sliced onion, tomato roses and cherry tomatoes. Serve hot with pickle and rice.

Rara Mutton
Curried Saddle of Lamb (Punjab)   *Serves: 6–8*

1.5 kg (3 lb) saddle of lamb or
  forequarter
3 tablespoons oil or ghee
2 large onions, finely chopped
1 tablespoon finely chopped
  fresh ginger
1 tablespoon finely chopped
  garlic
9 cardamom pods, bruised
3 teaspoons ground coriander
2 teaspoons ground cummin
1½ teaspoons ground fennel
½ teaspoon ground black
  pepper
1 teaspoon chilli powder or to
  taste

¼ cup ground cashews or
  almonds
4 ripe tomatoes, peeled and
  chopped
1 cup yoghurt
3 teaspoons salt
1 tablespoon lemon juice

Garnish:
3 tablespoons chopped fresh
  coriander

'Rara' means saddle and the name of this dish implies that the choicest portion of the saddle is used, but in fact the forequarter yields a greater proportion of meat to bone, and less fat, so is recommended.

Ask the butcher to cut the saddle or forequarter into chops, and each chop into 2 or 3 pieces.

Heat the oil or ghee in a large, heavy pan and fry the onions, ginger, garlic and cardamom pods, stirring frequently, until onions are soft and golden. Add the ground spices and nuts and fry for a minute longer, then add the tomatoes and stir well. Cover and simmer until tomatoes are pulpy. Beat the yoghurt with a fork until smooth, adding a little water if necessary, and add to the pan together with salt. Put in the meat, stir well, cover and cook until tender and the gravy thick and dark. Garnish with fresh coriander and serve with rice or chapatis.

Keema Alu Kari
Minced Meat and Potato Curry (Punjab)   *Serves: 4–6*

3 tablespoons oil or ghee
2 medium onions, finely
  chopped
1 teaspoon finely chopped
  garlic
1 teaspoon finely grated fresh
  ginger
½ teaspoon ground turmeric
2 teaspoons ground coriander
1 teaspoon ground cummin
½ teaspoon chilli powder,
  optional
2 teaspoons salt

2 tablespoons lemon juice or
  vinegar
500 g (1 lb) minced lamb or beef
500 g (1 lb) potatoes, peeled and
  quartered
1 cup hot water
1 teaspoon garam masala
  (page xxx)

Garnish:
2 tablespoons chopped fresh
  mint or coriander

Heat oil or ghee in a heavy saucepan and fry the onions, garlic and ginger until soft and golden. Add turmeric, coriander, cummin, chilli powder, if used, and fry, stirring, for 1 minute. Add the salt and lemon juice or vinegar and when it starts to sizzle fry the meat, stirring constantly, until all the meat is browned and any lumps broken up. Add the potatoes and hot water, bring to simmering point, cover and cook on low heat until potatoes are done and meat tender, about 30 minutes. Stir occasionally towards end of this time to ensure curry does not stick on base of pan. Sprinkle the garam masala over, stir gently, then serve garnished with the chopped herbs.

Palak Gosht
Spinach and Meat Curry (Punjab)   *Serves: 4*

500 g (1 lb) mutton or lamb
500 g (1 lb) spinach
4 tablespoons oil or ghee
½ teaspoon black cummin seeds
1 large onion
1 tablespoon chopped fresh
  ginger
2½ teaspoons chopped garlic

4 dried red chillies
2 teaspoons salt
1 bay leaf
3 cardamom pods, bruised
½ cup yoghurt
¼ teaspoon ground black
  pepper

Trim off all excess fat and cut meat into small cubes. Wash the spinach well and chop roughly. Peel and roughly chop the onion and put it into electric blender with ginger, garlic and chillies. (Break chillies into pieces and shake out the seeds if you prefer the flavour to be less hot.) Blend to a smooth purée, adding a little water, if necessary, to facilitate blending.

Heat oil or ghee in a heavy saucepan and fry the black cummin seeds for 1 minute. Add the blended mixture and fry, stirring, until it browns and the oil separates from the mixture, about 8–10 minutes. Add the meat and stir well. Cover and cook on low heat until juices come from the meat, then uncover and stir until liquid is almost absorbed. Add the spinach, salt, bay leaf and cardamoms. Stir well, cover and cook until liquid that comes from the spinach is absorbed. This will take about 1 hour, after which the meat should be quite tender.

Remove from heat, stir in yoghurt and pepper and serve hot with chapatis or puris.

Seekh Kebab
Minced Meat on Skewers (North India)   *Serves: 6*

750 g (1½ lb) finely minced lamb
1 teaspoon crushed garlic
1 teaspoon finely grated fresh ginger
2 teaspoons salt
1½ teaspoons garam masala (page 19)
2 tablespoons roasted chick peas, ground, or besan (chick pea flour)

2 tablespoons ground almonds
2 tablespoons finely chopped fresh coriander
1 fresh green chilli, seeded and finely chopped
2 tablespoons yoghurt
1 tablespoon lemon juice

Combine all the ingredients and mix thoroughly, kneading well until mixture becomes very smooth. Divide between 6 skewers and shape into long sausages. (Use skewers that are rectangular in cross-section, because the mixture will slip on round skewers.) Cook over glowing coals on a barbecue or under a preheated grill until browned on all sides and cooked through. Serve with rice or Indian bread, or as part of a waswan feast (see page 111).

Hussaini Kebab
Skewered Barbecued Lamb (North India)   *Serves: 6*

2 kg (4 lb) leg of lamb, boned
1 teaspoon crushed garlic
1½ teaspoons finely grated fresh
  ginger
1 teaspoon freshly ground black
  pepper
2 tablespoons finely ground
  almonds

2 tablespoons yoghurt
1 teaspoon ground coriander
1 teaspoon ground cummin
2½ teaspoons salt
2 tablespoons sesame oil
1 tablespoon lemon juice

Trim lamb, discarding excess fat. Any sinewy bits may be saved for
stock or for adding to a curry. Cut the lean meat into 2.5 cm (1 inch)
cubes and put into a large bowl.

Combine all the remaining ingredients, mixing well. Marinate
lamb in the mixture, kneading the spices well into the meat. Cover
and leave for 2 or 3 hours, or refrigerate and leave for as long as 4 days.

Thread 4 or 5 pieces of meat on each skewer and cook over
glowing coals or under a preheated grill until crisp and brown all
over, turning to ensure lamb is well cooked. Serve with parathas and
sas (page 138).

Kid Josh
Curried Lamb with Cashews and Coconut Milk
(Maharashtra Parsi)   *Serves: 6*

1 kg (2 lb) leg of lamb
250 g (8 oz) raw cashews
3 teaspoons chopped fresh
  ginger
5 teaspoons chopped garlic
10 fresh green chillies, seeded
1 teaspoon ground cinnamon

¼ teaspoon ground cloves
1½ teaspoons salt
4 tablespoons oil
approximately 2 cups hot water
1½ cups coconut milk
  (page xxxv)
4 large potatoes, quartered and
  fried

Trim all fat off lamb, and cut the meat into large cubes. In electric
blender grind the cashews finely and set aside. Put ginger, garlic and
chillies into the electric blender and blend to a purée, adding a little
water to facilitate blending. To the blended mixture add cinnamon,

cloves and salt. Mix half this mixture with the meat and set aside for half an hour.

Heat half the oil in a large, heavy saucepan and fry the meat until it changes colour. Pour in approximately 2 cups hot water, cover and cook on low heat until meat is tender and stock reduced to about 1 cup.

In another saucepan heat remaining oil and fry the rest of the blended mixture, stirring, until it changes colour and starts to stick slightly at base of pan. Add ground cashews, coconut milk and stock and simmer, stirring for a few minutes. Add meat and let it simmer until oil rises to the top. Do not cover pan after adding coconut milk. Serve hot with the fried potatoes, and accompanied by hot boiled rice.

Tabak Maaz
Spiced Ribs of Lamb (Kashmir)   *Serves: 6–8*

1.5 kg (3 lb) ribs of lamb
1 teaspoon chopped garlic
3 tablespoons chopped fresh
  coriander
½ cup milk
1½ cups water
1 teaspoon ground turmeric
1 teaspoon chilli powder

½ teaspoon ground cardamom
½ teaspoon ground fennel
¼ teaspoon ground black
  pepper
2 teaspoons salt
1½ cups water
1 teaspoon ghee
1 tablespoon oil

Ask the butcher to remove all excess fat and cut the lamb ribs in short lengths, two or three ribs to a piece.

Combine the garlic, coriander and milk in electric blender, mix in the ground spices and salt. Put into pressure cooker with meat and water. Bring to pressure and cook for 15 minutes. Turn off heat, allow pressure to drop, then open pan and cook until almost all liquid has evaporated. Alternatively put in saucepan with water to cover and cook until tender. Take ribs from pan and allow to drain. In a heavy frying pan heat the ghee and oil and shallow fry the pieces of lamb ribs, pressing them down against the pan with a frying slice so that they get nicely browned. Drain on absorbent paper, serve hot. The ends of the ribs may be decorated with silver foil. Any liquid left after boiling the ribs may be reduced to make a delicious sauce once the fat has been spooned off.

Methi Maaz

Mutton with Fenugreek (Kashmir)   *Serves: 6*

2 bunches fresh fenugreek or
  1 bunch spinach
500 g (1 lb) lamb
3 tablespoons ghee or mustard
  oil
1 large onion, finely chopped
1 teaspoon finely chopped
  garlic

2 teaspoons finely chopped
  fresh ginger
1 teaspoon chilli powder, or to
  taste
1 teaspoon ground turmeric
2 ripe tomatoes, peeled and
  chopped
2 teaspoons salt
1 teaspoon Kashmiri garam
  masala (page xxx)

*If you cannot get fresh fenugreek herb, use spinach as a substitute
and give it flavour by adding 2 tablespoons of dried fenugreek leaves.*

Wash the greens well and discard any tough stalks. Cut the meat
into small cubes. Heat ghee or oil and gently fry onion, garlic and
ginger until soft and golden. Add chilli powder and turmeric, stir,
then add meat to the pan and fry, stirring, until the colour changes.
Add tomatoes and salt and a little water. Cover and simmer on very
low heat until meat is almost tender. If liquid evaporates, add a little
hot water. Add the fresh fenugreek or spinach and dried fenugreek,
sprinkle with garam masala and continue cooking until greens are
cooked to a pulp, the meat completely tender and oil comes to the
surface. Serve hot with rice or chapatis.

Pasanda Kebab

Fried Lamb Rolls (Hyderabad)   *Serves: 4*

500 g (1 lb) lean lamb from leg
2 teaspoons chopped fresh
  ginger
3 teaspoons chopped garlic
1 tablespoon cummin seeds,
  lightly roasted in dry pan
3 fresh green chillies, seeded
2 dried red chillies, preferably
  Kashmiri chillies

1 teaspoon salt
1 teaspoon Kashmiri garam
  masala (page xxx)
1 medium onion, roughly
  chopped
2 teaspoons ground coriander
2 tablespoons ghee or oil for
  frying

Cut lamb into very thin slices and beat lightly on one side with a meat mallet, to flatten. These are pasandas.

Put all other ingredients except ghee into electric blender. Blend to a paste and apply to both sides of each piece of meat. Leave for at least 1 hour for flavours to penetrate. Roll up each pasanda and tie with string or fasten with a wooden toothpick.

Heat ghee or oil in a heavy frying pan and fry the pasandas on a medium heat until brown. Cover and cook 10 minutes or place on barbecue or under grill to finish cooking.

Note: In India if meat is not of premium quality, a small piece of green pawpaw is added to the marinade to act as a meat tenderiser.

Gurda Kari
Kidney Curry (Punjab)   *Serves: 6*

8 lambs' kidneys
1 teaspoon finely grated fresh ginger
1 teaspoon crushed garlic
1 teaspoon chilli powder or to taste
1 teaspoon garam masala (page xxx)
2 tablespoons ghee or oil
2 medium onions, finely chopped

2 ripe tomatoes, peeled and diced
1½ teaspoons salt
1 cup yoghurt

Garnish:
3 hard boiled eggs, optional

Cut kidneys in halves lengthways, remove core, then cut each half into 3 or 4 pieces. Combine with ginger, garlic, chilli powder and garam masala and marinate for about 1 hour.

Heat ghee or oil in heavy saucepan and fry the onions until soft and starting to brown. Add the kidneys and fry until they change colour. Add tomatoes, salt and enough water to almost cover the kidneys. Cover and simmer until kidneys are tender, about 35 minutes. Beat the yoghurt with a fork until smooth, adding a little water if it is thick. Stir it into the curry and heat through. Serve hot. This dish may be garnished with hard boiled eggs cut in slices or wedges. It goes well with plain boiled rice.

Mutton Kari

Madras Style Meat Curry (South India)   *Serves: 6*

1.5 kg (3 lb) lamb forequater
  chops or other meat, cubed
3 tablespoons oil
10 curry leaves
3 medium onions, finely
  chopped
3 teaspoons chopped garlic
1 tablespoon finely chopped
  fresh ginger
1 teaspoon ground turmeric
3–4 teaspoons chilli powder,
  or to taste

3 teaspoons ground coriander
1 teaspoon ground cummin
2½ teaspoons salt
2 tablespoons vinegar
2 tablespoons desiccated
  coconut
1½ cups coconut milk
  (page xxxv)
2 or 3 fresh green chillies, split
  halfway from tip

*Hotter than North Indian dishes, the curries of the south seem to
require the pungency of chillies and pepper to stimulate heat-jaded
appetites. The secret of being able to eat a hot curry is to combine it
with rice, in the proportion of at least four parts rice to one of curry.*

Cut chops in large pieces, keeping the bone in. Heat oil in a large
heavy saucepan and fry the curry leaves until brown. Add onions,
garlic and ginger and fry until soft and golden. Add turmeric and fry
for a few seconds, then put in chilli powder, coriander and cummin
and fry for 1 minute.

   Add salt and vinegar and stir until liquid evaporates, then put in
the meat and stir until it is coated with the spices. Add green
chillies, lower heat, cover and cook until meat is tender. Juices come
from the meat and there should be no need to add water.

   Meanwhile, roast the coconut in a dry pan until golden brown.
Grind in electric blender until finely ground and if necessary add ½
cup of the coconut milk to facilitate blending. Blend at high speed
for 30 seconds. Add to the curry together with the rest of the
coconut milk and simmer uncovered until gravy is thick. Serve with
rice and accompaniments.

Sorpotel
Pork and Liver Curry (Goan Christian)   *Serves: 6–8*

1 kg (2 lb) pork from leg or
   shoulder
250 g (8 oz) pork or calves
   liver
10–15 dried red chillies,
   preferably Kashmiri or Goan
   chillies
1 cup vinegar, preferably
   coconut vinegar
2 or 3 fresh green chillies
2 tablespoons chopped
   ginger

2 tablespoons chopped garlic
½ teaspoon ground black
   pepper
2 teaspoons ground coriander
2 teaspoons ground cummin
1 teaspoon ground turmeric
1 teaspoon ground cinnamon
½ teaspoon ground cloves
2 teaspoons salt
1 tablespoon tamarind pulp or
   1 teaspoon instant tamarind
½ cup hot water
1 teaspoon sugar

Put the pork into a saucepan with just enough lightly salted water to
cover, bring to the boil and simmer on low heat for 5 minutes. Cook
the liver separately in the same way. Discard stock from the liver,
allow liver to cool and cut it into very tiny dice. Reserve the pork
stock and cut the pork, together with its skin and fat, into larger dice.

Discard stalks of the dried chillies. If a less hot curry is preferred
discard the seeds as well. Soak the dried chillies in the vinegar for
about 10 minutes. Put dried chillies, vinegar, roughly chopped
green chillies, ginger and garlic into electric blender and blend until
smooth. Add the ground spices and salt. Put pork, pork stock, diced
liver and the blended spices into an enamel or stainless steel
saucepan and simmer, covered, until pork is tender, about 1 hour.
Meanwhile soak tamarind pulp in hot water for a few minutes,
squeeze to dissolve the pulp and strain through a fine sieve. Discard
seeds and fibres. Alternatively dissolve instant tamarind in hot
water. Add the tamarind liquid and sugar and continue cooking,
uncovered, until gravy is thick and dark. Serve with plain boiled rice.

Shikar Vindaloo
Pork Vinegar Curry (Goan Christian)   *Serves: 6–8*

1 kg (2 lb) pork
6–8 large dried red chillies
1 cup vinegar, preferably
  coconut vinegar
2 teaspoons chopped fresh
  ginger
4 teaspoons chopped garlic
2 teaspoons ground cummin
½ teaspoon ground black
  pepper

½ teaspoon ground cinnamon
½ teaspoon ground cardamom
¼ teaspoon ground cloves
¼ teaspoon ground nutmeg
2 teaspoons salt
2–3 tablespoons ghee or oil
2 medium onions, finely
  chopped
1 tablespoon brown sugar

Cut pork into cubes. Soak chillies in vinegar for 10 minutes. If available use coconut vinegar for authentic flavour, but any kind of vinegar may be substituted, diluting it if it is very strong. Put chillies and vinegar, ginger, garlic, all the ground spices and salt into electric blender and blend until chillies are finely ground. Pour this mixture over the pork in an earthenware bowl, cover and marinate for 2 hours.

Heat enough ghee or oil to cover base of an enamel or stainless steel saucepan. (This dish is cooked in earthenware pots in India and if one is available it would be an advantage.) Fry the onions on low heat until soft and golden, stirring frequently. Drain pork from the marinade and fry on medium high heat, stirring, until it changes colour. Pour in marinade, cover pan and simmer on low heat until pork is tender, about 1½ hours. Stir in sugar. Serve with plain boiled rice.

Kofta Kari
Meatball Curry (Punjab)

Meatballs:
750 g (1½ lb) finely minced lamb
1 medium onion, finely
  chopped
½ teaspoon crushed garlic
½ teaspoon finely grated fresh
  ginger
1 fresh red or green chilli,
  seeded and finely chopped
3 tablespoons chopped fresh
  coriander or mint
1½ teaspoons salt
1 teaspoon garam masala
  (page xxx)

Gravy:
3 tablespoons ghee or oil
2 medium onions, finely
  chopped
1 teaspoon finely chopped garlic
1 tablespoon finely chopped
  fresh ginger
1 teaspoon ground turmeric
1 teaspoon garam masala
  (page xxx)
1 teaspoon chilli powder
2 ripe tomatoes, peeled and
  chopped
1 teaspoon salt
2 tablespoons chopped
  coriander or mint
lemon juice to taste

Meatballs: Mix minced lamb thoroughly with all the other ingredients. Shape into small balls.

Gravy: Heat ghee or oil in a large, heavy saucepan, brown the meatballs, remove from pan and set aside. In the same pan fry the onions, garlic and ginger until soft and golden. Add turmeric, garam masala and chilli powder, fry for 1 minute. Add tomatoes, salt and meatballs, cover and simmer for 25 minutes or until gravy is thick and meatballs soft. Stir in chopped herbs and lemon juice. Serve with rice or chapatis.

Kaleji Kari

Liver Curry (Kerala)   *Serves: 4*

3 tablespoons coconut or other vegetable oil
8 curry leaves
2 medium onions, finely chopped
2 teaspoons finely chopped garlic
1 teaspoon finely chopped fresh ginger
2 fresh red or green chillies, seeded and chopped

2 teaspoons ground coriander
1 teaspoon ground cummin
½ teaspoon ground turmeric
1 teaspoon chilli powder or to taste
500 g (1 lb) liver, diced
1½ cups coconut milk (page xxxv)
1 teaspoon salt
2 tablespoons lemon juice

Heat the oil in a heavy saucepan and fry the curry leaves, onions, garlic, ginger and chillies over medium heat, stirring frequently, until the onions are golden brown. Add the coriander, cummin, turmeric and chilli powder and fry for about 1 minute, stirring constantly. Add the liver and stir until the colour changes. Add coconut milk and salt and simmer uncovered until liver is tender and gravy thick. Remove from pan and add lemon juice. Serve hot with plain boiled rice.

Accompaniments

Even the simplest Indian meal includes a variety of accompaniments. They are intended to tempt the appetite, and they do this in different ways. There are strong tasting items like Bombay duck and fresh flavoured chutneys made from herbs like coriander and mint. There are crisp *pappadams* for texture contrast and *raitas* and *pachchadis* based on yoghurt to act as coolers in contrast to the hot and piquant pickles.

Some accompaniments such as *piaz sambal* are as simple as sliced onion sprinkled with salt, chilli powder and a squeeze of lime or lemon juice, but they add greatly to the food they are eaten with. Most accompaniments are made freshly for each meal, but there are some pickles and chutneys which keep well.

Green mangoes and other fruit are associated with the sweet chutneys so popular with Western tastes, but Indians favour oil pickles such as the chilli pickle which are pungent instead of sweet.

Kachumbar
Onion, Tomato and Chilli Salad (Maharashtra Parsi)   *Serves: 6*

2 medium onions
salt
1 tablespoon tamarind pulp or
   1 teaspoon instant tamarind
½ cup hot water
2 tablespoons brown sugar or
   jaggery
2 firm ripe tomatoes

1 tablespoon finely shredded
   fresh ginger
2 or 3 fresh red or green chillies,
   seeded and sliced
2 tablespoons chopped fresh
   coriander

Peel the onions, cut them in halves lengthways and then cut across into fine slices. Sprinkle generously with salt and leave for 1 hour. Press out all the liquid and rinse once in cold water. Drain well. Soak tamarind pulp in hot water for a few minutes, then squeeze to dissolve pulp and strain, discarding the seeds. If using instant tamarind, dissolve in the hot water. Dissolve sugar or jaggery in the tamarind liquid.

Scald tomatoes, peel and dice. Combine all the ingredients, add salt to taste, chill and serve. Salads of this type are not served on their own, but as accompaniments to rice, curries or main dishes.

Khira Raita
Yoghurt with Cucumbers (Punjab)   *Serves: 6*

2 green cucumbers
2 teaspoons salt
2 tablespoons finely chopped
   spring onion
1½ cups yoghurt
lemon juice to taste
1½ teaspoons cummin seeds

Garnish:
1 tablespoon chopped fresh
   coriander or mint

Peel the cucumbers, halve them lengthways and remove the seeds. Cut the cucumbers into small dice, sprinkle with salt and leave for 15 minutes, then drain away liquid and rinse the cucumbers quickly in cold water. Drain well. Combine with onion, yoghurt, lemon juice and taste to see if more salt is required. Roast the cummin seeds in a dry pan, shaking pan or stirring constantly, until brown. Bruise or crush seeds and sprinkle over yoghurt. Serve chilled, garnished with mint or coriander.

Palak Pachchadi
Yoghurt with Spinach   *Serves: 4–6*

1 large bunch spinach
2 teaspoons ghee or oil
1 teaspoon black mustard seeds
1 teaspoon cummin seeds
1 teaspoon ground cummin

½ teaspoon fenugreek seeds
⅛ teaspoon chilli powder,
   optional
¾ teaspoon salt or to taste
1½ cups yoghurt

Wash spinach thoroughly in several changes of water. Remove any tough stems and put the leaves into a saucepan with very little water. Cover and steam over low heat until spinach is tender. Drain and chop finely.

   In a small pan heat ghee or oil and fry the mustard seeds until they start to pop. Add cummin seeds, ground cummin and fenugreek seeds and continue to fry, stirring with a wooden spoon, until the fenugreek seeds are golden brown, but do not allow to burn. Remove from heat, stir in chilli powder, if used, and salt and allow to cool. Mix in the yoghurt, then stir this mixture into the spinach. Serve cold or at room temperature as a side dish with rice and curry, or with one of the Indian breads.

Dahi Kachumbar
Yoghurt and Onion Salad (Maharashtra Parsi)   *Serves: 6*

3 medium onions
1 teaspoon salt
1 cup yoghurt
1 teaspoon finely grated fresh
   ginger

2 medium tomatoes, peeled and
   chopped
3 fresh green chillies, seeded
   and chopped
3 tablespoons chopped fresh
   coriander

Cut the onions into thin slices, sprinkle with the salt and set aside for 20 minutes. Squeeze out as much liquid as possible. Mix together the yoghurt and ginger, then fold in the onions and the rest of the ingredients. Cover and chill thoroughly before serving.

Piaz Sambal
Onion Sambal

2 medium onions, preferably
   red onions
$\frac{1}{2}$ teaspoon chilli powder

$\frac{1}{2}$ teaspoon salt or to taste
lime or lemon juice to taste

Peel and finely slice the onions. Sprinkle with chilli powder, salt and lemon juice. Toss lightly until well mixed and serve as an accompaniment to rice and curries. Make this sambal just before serving.

Kela Raita
Yoghurt with Bananas   *Serves: 6*

4 large ripe bananas
lemon juice
1 teaspoon cummin seeds
1 cup yoghurt

3 tablespoons freshly grated or
   desiccated coconut
$\frac{1}{2}$ teaspoon salt
2 teaspoons sugar

Slice the bananas and sprinkle with lemon juice. Roast cummin seeds in a dry pan, shaking or stirring constantly until brown. Crush or grind. Combine the yoghurt with all the ingredients except the banana. If desiccated coconut is used, moisten it first by sprinkling with about 2 tablespoons water and tossing it with the fingers until it is no longer dry. Fold banana into yoghurt mixture. Chill and serve.

Sas
Saffron and Cream Sauce (North India)   *Serves: 6*

¹/₈ teaspoon saffron strands
2 tablespoons boiling water
2 tablespoons blanched
   pistachios
4 tablespoons blanched
   almonds
1 tablespoon ghee or butter

³/₄ cup cream
¹/₂ cup milk
¹/₄ teaspoon ground cardamom
¹/₂ teaspoon salt or to taste
¹/₂ teaspoon white pepper

Pound saffron in mortar and pestle, then dissolve in the boiling water. Put pistachios and almonds into electric blender and grind finely, or pound with mortar and pestle. Heat the ghee or butter in a small pan and fry the ground nuts, stirring constantly. Add the saffron, cream, milk, cardamom, salt and pepper and simmer, stirring constantly, until sauce is thick. Serve with kebabs.

Masala Papad
Pappadams with Garnish (Maharashtra)   *Serves: 6*

6 large pappadams
oil for deep frying
¹/₂ cup freshly grated coconut

2 tablespoons finely chopped
   fresh coriander
chilli powder to taste

These dried lentil wafers are sold in packets.

Heat oil in karahi or deep frying pan and fry the pappadams one at a time for just a few seconds, until they swell and turn golden. Drain on absorbent paper. Sprinkle each one with the coconut, coriander and chilli powder and serve at once, as an accompaniment to rice and curries.

Podina Chatni
Fresh Mint Chutney

1 cup firmly packed mint leaves
6 spring onions, including
    green leaves
2 fresh green chillies, roughly
    chopped
½ teaspoon chopped garlic,
    optional

1 teaspoon salt
2 teaspoons sugar
1 teaspoon garam masala
    (page xxx)
⅓ cup lemon juice
2 tablespoons water

In the absence of the grinding stones which are used in India for reducing grains to flour and others which make 'wet' masalas and fresh chutneys, a powerful electric blender is the Western cook's best friend when preparing Indian food.

Put mint into blender together with onions cut into short lengths and all other ingredients. Blend on high speed to a smooth purée. If blender is not available, finely chop mint, onions and chillies and pound a little at a time in mortar and pestle, then mix in remaining ingredients.

Pack the chutney into a small dish, smooth the surface, cover and chill. Serve as an accompaniment with rice and curries, chapatis, thosai (page 11) and other savouries such as samosa.

Am Chatni
Green Mango Chutney

1 large green mango
½ teaspoon salt

½ teaspoon chilli powder or
    to taste

Peel and slice the mango thinly and cut it into fine slivers. Toss with the salt and chilli powder and serve as an accompaniment to a curry meal, or as an appetizer at the start of a meal.

Note: Tart green cooking apples may be used instead of mango.

Nariyal Chatni
Coconut Chutney (Tamil Nadu)   *Serves: 6–8*

½ fresh coconut, grated or 1 cup
   desiccated coconut
1 lemon or lime
2 or 3 fresh red or green chillies
1 teaspoon salt
2 teaspoons ghee or oil

⅛ teaspoon ground asafoetida,
   optional
1 teaspoon black mustard seeds
1 teaspoon black cummin seeds
10 curry leaves
½ teaspoon urad dhal (page 62)

If using desiccated coconut, sprinkle with about ¼ cup water and
toss to moisten evenly. Peel the lemon or lime so that no white pith
remains. Cut in pieces and remove the seeds. Put into electric
blender with the seeded and roughly chopped chillies and blend
until smooth. Add the coconut and continue blending to a smooth
paste, scraping down sides of blender and adding a little more
liquid if necessary. Add the salt and mix.

Heat ghee or oil in a small pan and fry the remaining ingredients,
stirring frequently, until mustard seeds pop and dhal is golden. Mix
with the blended mixture, pat into a flat cake and serve with thosai
(page 11), or as an accompaniment to a rice meal.

Dhania ki Nariyal Chatni
Fresh Coriander and Coconut Chutney   *Serves: 6*

1 cup fresh coriander
2 tablespoons desiccated
   coconut
3 tablespoons water
1 teaspoon chopped garlic

1 fresh green chilli, seeded
1 teaspoon garam masala
   (page xxx)
1 teaspoon salt
2 tablespoons lemon juice

Put the well-washed coriander into electric blender with all other
ingredients and blend on high speed until smooth. If necessary, add
a little water to facilitate blending, but do not make the mixture too
wet.

Imli Chatni
Tamarind Chutney

3 tablespoons dried tamarind
   pulp
1 cup hot water
1 teaspoon salt
2 teaspoons jaggery or brown
   sugar

1 teaspoon ground cummin
½ teaspoon ground fennel
2 teaspoons finely grated fresh
   ginger
lemon juice to taste
pinch chilli powder, optional

Put tamarind pulp in a bowl with hot water and allow to soak until water is cool. Knead and squeeze pulp away from the seeds until it is dissolved in the water, then strain through a fine nylon sieve, pushing all the pulp through. If necessary, add a little more water to assist in getting all the pulp from the seeds. Add salt, sugar and other ingredients to the tamarind and stir to mix well. Taste and add more salt if necessary, lemon juice to sharpen the flavour and, if liked, a small pinch of chilli powder.

Mirich Achar
Chilli Pickle (Maharashtra)

1 kg (2 lb) long green chillies
2 tablespoons salt
1 tablespoon ground turmeric
1½ tablespoons black mustard
   seed
¼ cup vinegar

2 tablespoons chopped garlic
2 cups mustard oil
1 teaspoon fenugreek seeds
2 teaspoons black cummin
   seeds
2 teaspoons crushed asafoetida

Wash chillies well and rub dry in tea towel. Cut off and discard stalks, slice chillies crossways into 1 cm (½ inch) slices. Sprinkle with salt and turmeric, toss well to mix, cover and leave for 2 days, preferably in the sun for a few hours each day. Soak the mustard seed in the vinegar overnight, and next day grind in electric blender together with the garlic to form a purée.

Heat oil in a large pan and add the fenugreek seeds and black cummin seeds. Stir and fry until fenugreek is golden brown, then add the asafoetida, stir once, and add the blended mixture and the chillies together with liquid that comes from them. Cook and stir occasionally until oil rises and chillies are cooked. They should not be too soft. Cool and put into sterilised bottle.

Baigan Kasaundi
Aubergine Pickle

1 kg (2 lb) aubergines
12 dried red chillies
4 teaspoons chopped garlic
3 teaspoons chopped fresh
  ginger
2 tablespoons black mustard
  seeds
1½ teaspoons ground turmeric

1½ cups oil
3 teaspoons salt
½ cup brown sugar or chopped
  jaggery
¾ cup vinegar
2 teaspoons garam masala
  (page xxx)

Wash aubergines and cut crossways into slices. If aubergines are very large, cut into cubes. Soak chillies in hot water for 5 minutes. In electric blender combine chillies, garlic, ginger, mustard seeds and some of the water in which the chillies soaked. Blend on high speed until puréed. If blender is not available, pound in mortar and pestle. Combine with turmeric.

Heat the oil and fry the blended mixture for a few minutes, then add aubergine, cover and cook on low heat until aubergine is soft, stirring now and then. Add salt, sugar and vinegar and simmer until thick, stirring to prevent burning. Stir in garam masala, remove from heat. Cool and bottle.

Lagan Nu Achar
Wedding Pickle (Maharashtra Parsi)

½ cup chopped dates
½ cup raisins
½ cup chopped dried apricots
½ cup chopped dried figs
1 cup water
500 g (1 lb) carrots
1 teaspoon cummin seeds
2 small cinnamon sticks
1 teaspoon ground cardamom

¼ teaspoon ground cloves
2 cups vinegar
2 cups chopped jaggery or
  brown sugar
3 teaspoons salt
2 teaspoons chilli powder
2 teaspoons ground black
  mustard
1 teaspoon crushed garlic
1 teaspoon grated fresh ginger

This fruit pickle is traditionally served at Parsi weddings. I tasted it first at the famous Fariyas Hotel in Bombay, where talented Parsi cooks invited me to lunch on some of their most celebrated dishes.

Soak dried fruits in water for 1 hour. Wash and scrape the carrots and grate on fine grater. Put all the ingredients into a stainless steel or enamel pan and bring slowly to the boil, stirring. Simmer until the fruit is very soft and the liquid syrupy. Cool and store in sterilised bottles. Remove cinnamon sticks before serving.

Boomla
Bombay Duck (Maharashtra)

A pungent dried fish which is served as an accompaniment to rice and curry meals. Sold in packets, the fish should be cut into pieces about 5 cm (2 inch) in length and deep fried in hot oil until light golden brown. Drain and serve as a crisp nibble between mouthfuls of rice.

An alternative method is to fry finely sliced onions in some of the oil after the Bombay ducks are fried, and, if liked, some broken dried red chillies to be fried together with the onions. Fry on low heat, stirring, until onions are golden brown. Add a little salt and sugar, stir well, combine with the fried Bombay duck and serve as a sambal.

Drinks, Desserts and Sweetmeats

Thinking back on a wonderful trip through India, I recall how very appropriate the drinks were at each stage of the journey.

In the misty beginning of winter in Kashmir a bubbling *samovar* was always brought to the table after a meal and topaz coloured tea poured into small bowls. The bowls already held flaked almonds and the tea was fragrant with cinnamon, cardamom and the world's most precious spice, saffron. Warming one's hands on the bowl was part of the charm of being served tea in this fashion and the spicy liquid seemed to complement the rich Kashmiri food.

It was in Kashmir too that I was introduced to an aperitif that at first startles, then grows on you – a peppery, salty concoction called *jal jeera*. Perhaps easier to get accustomed to is *zeera pani*, a refreshingly tart drink flavoured with cummin and tamarind.

In hotter parts of the country, *nimboo pani* (lime juice) was the order of the day, either sweetened or salted. The lightly salted version is more thirst quenching, but I liked the sweetened juice with a generous pinch of salt added. Try adding salt (just enough to be tasted) to any citrus juice, pineapple juice, or combination of fruit juices – it brings out the flavour.

In sunkissed Goa on the west coast of India, the cool, sweet juice of fresh young coconuts is top favourite. Here coconut palms grow everywhere, particularly along the beaches where the sand is fine and silky soft, golden in the sunlight and silvery by moonlight.

At the lovely Fort Aguada Beach Resort we listened to a trio singing and playing lilting Portuguese-influenced music and sipped long refreshing drinks that combined coconut juice, feni, crushed ice and a touch of lime juice right in the coconut shell. Feni, a locally produced liquor made from the cashew fruit, is clear and colourless and packs a kick like a mule. Be wary.

The best part of finishing a young coconut (with or without added ingredients) is scooping out the tender, creamy flesh and enjoying its extremely delicate flavour.

Throughout India a very popular beverage is *lassi*, a drink of unflavoured yoghurt beaten smooth and mixed with water and ice, either sweetened or salted. Sweet cold drinks called *sharbat* are also popular and the flavours are really exotic. In the lavish, white marble surroundings of the Hotel Mughal in Agra, my thoughts still full of my first sight of the Taj Mahal by moonlight, a sandalwood *sharbat* seemed quite appropriate. However, rose flavour is perhaps most popular.

Indians seem to have a collective sweet tooth but desserts are not always part of a meal. If a sweet is served, it is surprising to the Westerner that it may be served at the start of the meal (to sweeten the mouth) or placed on the *thali* (individual serving tray) together with the savoury dishes. One does not necessarily have to eat it at the end of the meal.

There are literally dozens of varieties of sweetmeats in India. Most are based on concentrated milk products, almonds or lentils so they are considered not just an indulgence, but strengthening and beneficial to health. Almonds, in particular, are supposed to help one's ability to concentrate and are fed to examination students.

While Indian sweets may be strange to those conditioned to lollipops and chocolate bars, most people enjoy the spicy flavours and contrasting textures that make discovering new varieties such an adventure.

Falooda
Rose-flavoured Milk Sherbet

agar-agar jelly, diced (see below)
rose syrup as in sharbat gulab
   (page 150)
ice cold milk as required, about
   1 cup for each serving
crushed ice
2 teaspoons soaked tulsi seeds,
   optional

Jelly:
3 cups water
4 teaspoons agar-agar powder or
   1 cup soaked agar-agar
   strands
6 tablespoons sugar
12 drops rose essence
1 teaspoon liquid red food
   colouring
1 teaspoon liquid green food
   colouring

There are many versions of falooda – this one is a favourite. It is a sweet drink ideal for serving with curry meals. It gets its name from the particles of cornflour vermicelli that float in it but these, which are difficult to make without special equipment, are often replaced with tiny pieces of jelly or cooked tapioca. Another easy substitute is cellophane noodles (bean starch noodles) soaked and boiled until soft and transparent, then cut into short lengths.

Falooda can be served as a dessert or as a refreshing drink. In this version a rose-flavoured syrup is mixed with ice-cold milk, crushed ice and jewel-like squares of sparkling red and green agar-agar jelly in tall glasses.

Agar-agar can be bought in powder form by the gram or ounce from chemists, or in packets from Asian grocery stores, either powdered or in strands. It is popular in Asia for making jellies and sweetmeats because it sets without refrigeration.

Put about 2 tablespoons each of diced jelly and rose syrup into each tall glass, fill up with ice-cold milk and crushed ice. If liked, some soaked tulsi seeds can be floated on top.

Jelly: Measure water into a saucepan and sprinkle agar-agar powder over. If agar-agar strands are used, soak at least 2 hours in cold water, then drain and measure 1 cup loosely packed. Bring to the boil and simmer gently, stirring, until agar-agar dissolves. Powder takes about 10 minutes and the strands take longer, about 25–30 minutes. Add sugar and dissolve, remove from heat, cool slightly and add rose flavouring. Divide mixture between two large shallow dishes and colour one red and the other green. Leave to set. When quite cold and firm, cut with a sharp knife first into fine strips, then across into small dice.

Qahwah
Kashmiri Tea (Kashmir)

4 cups boiling water	pinch of saffron strands
1 teaspoon Kashmiri green tea	2 tablespoons finely flaked
4 cardamom pods, bruised	almonds
1 small piece cinnamon stick	sugar or honey to taste

Sitting around a bubbling samovar is one of the joys of a Kashmir winter. If you don't have a samovar, try it anyway, using a teapot, but give authenticity to the occasion by using little bowls (like Chinese rice bowls) instead of teacups with handles.

Prepare the samovar with coals in its central tube, or warm the teapot by letting it stand for a minute or two with boiling water in it. Rinse out, put in the tea and spices and pour the measured boiling water over. Allow to steep for 5 minutes.

In each bowl put a teaspoonful of almonds. Pour the tea over the almonds, sweeten to taste and drink hot.

Thandai
Almond Milk Drink (Punjab)   *Serves: 2*

20 almonds	1½ cups water
5 peppercorns	1 cup milk
2 teaspoons chaar magaz or	sugar to taste
sunflower seeds	rose water or essence to flavour

Nutrition experts tell us that almonds are rich in protein and are good value. The people of India seem to have known this instinctively for centuries, and incorporate almonds in sweet and savoury dishes. This refreshing drink is ideal when the weather is so hot that the appetite flags. The goodness of almonds and kernels of seeds is extracted by grinding them together with milk. Serve as a cool treat.

Blanch the almonds and put into electric blender with peppercorns, seeds and half the water. Blend at high speed until finely ground and strain into a jug through a fine clean muslin bag. Return the ground mixture left in the cloth to the blender with remaining water, blend again and once more extract the liquid. (The finely ground almond residue may be refrigerated or frozen and used for thickening curries.) Mix milk with the almond liquid, add sugar to taste and rose water or essence to flavour. Add crushed ice, or keep refrigerated until served. A pretty touch is to float a few small rose petals on top of the drink.

Lassi
Buttermilk or Yoghurt Drink (North India)   *Makes 4 servings*

2 cups buttermilk	salt and pepper to taste
2 cups iced water or	pinch of cummin, toasted and
1 cup yoghurt	ground, optional
3 cups iced water	

Mix equal parts of cultured buttermilk and iced water, or beat yoghurt until smooth and gradually stir in iced water. Season with salt, pepper and a pinch of toasted, ground cummin. Alternatively, sweeten lightly with sugar. Serve with ice.

Another yoghurt drink popular with children and adults is 2 tablespoons yoghurt beaten with 2 teaspoons of sugar in a tall glass, with iced soda or lemonade added. It will froth and look like a milk shake and even children who do not like yoghurt will find it acceptable.

In South India, buttermilk is served with more pungent flavouring including ginger, coriander leaves and green chillies ground to a paste.

Zeera Pani
Cummin and Tamarind Drink (Uttar Pradesh)   *Serves: 3–4*

½ cup dried tamarind pulp
2 cups hot water
3 teaspoons finely grated fresh
    ginger
2 teaspoons ground cummin
pinch chilli powder, optional
½ teaspoon garam masala
    (page xxx)
3 teaspoons sugar, or to taste
salt to taste
iced water and crushed ice

Garnish:
mint sprigs and lemon slices

Serve this drink by itself, as a refresher, or along with rice meals as a digestive. It may also be served at cocktail time as a non-alcoholic aperitif.

Soak tamarind pulp in the hot water and leave for 2 hours. Squeeze to dissolve the pulp and separate the seeds and fibres. Strain through a fine nylon sieve. Add remaining ingredients, stir well, then strain again through a very fine sieve or muslin. Chill. At serving time dilute to taste with iced water, add crushed ice and garnish with mint and sliced lemon.

Sharbat Gulab
Rose-flavoured Cold Drink (North India)

3 cups white sugar
2 cups water
20 drops rose essence
1 teaspoon liquid red food
  colouring

1 teaspoon tulsi seeds
iced water and crushed ice for
  serving

Put sugar and water in a saucepan and cook over gentle heat until sugar dissolves. Cool. Add rose flavouring and red colouring. Rose syrup should be a strong colour, for it will be mixed with a large proportion of water.

Soak the tulsi seeds in a cup of cold water. After a few minutes they will develop a jelly-like coating. (The seeds can be kept soaking in the refrigerator for a week. They are supposed to have a very cooling effect, and are used in almost every type of sharbat drink.)

At serving time put 2 tablespoons of syrup in each glass and fill up with iced water and crushed ice. Syrup can be increased or decreased according to taste. Add a spoonful of soaked tulsi seeds, stir in and serve.

Seviyan Kheer
Creamy Vermicelli Pudding (Punjab)   *Serves: 4*

5 cups milk
½ cup broken vermicelli
6 tablespoons sugar
2 tablespoons sultanas

¼ cup blanched, slivered
  almonds
2 drops kewra essence
1 tablespoon chopped pistachios

Bring milk to the boil, stirring constantly. Add the vermicelli and continue to cook until vermicelli is soft. Add the sugar, sultanas and almonds. Stir over medium heat until the mixture is like a thick custard. Remove from heat, add the flavouring and spoon into dessert dish or individual bowls. Decorate with pistachios. Serve warm or chilled.

Firni
Creamy Rice Blancmange (Punjab)   *Serves: 4*

3 cups milk
3 tablespoons ground rice
3 tablespoons sugar
½ teaspoon ground cardamom
1 tablespoon rose water or 2–3
  drops rose essence

2 tablespoons blanched
  pistachios or almonds
red food colouring, optional
edible silver leaf (varak),
  optional

Mix a little of the milk with the ground rice to form a smooth cream. Bring the rest of the milk to the boil with sugar, stirring with a wooden spoon. Remove from heat and stir in the ground rice, then return pan to heat and stir constantly until the mixture boils and thickens. Boil, stirring, for 3–5 minutes. Remove from heat, sprinkle in the cardamom, rose flavouring and half the nuts, finely chopped. Pour into individual dessert dishes and decorate tops with the remaining nuts, ground or slivered. For special occasions tint the firni a pale rose pink or decorate the top with varak (edible silver leaf, available from Indian specialty grocers). Chill for a few hours before serving. In winter, however, this sweet may be served warm.

Panchamrit
Creamed Rice and Bananas (Karnataka)   *Serves: 6*

1 cup flaked rice (powva or phoa)
3 cups milk
3 tablespoons sugar

¼ teaspoon ground cardamom
2 tablespoons ghee
3 soft ripe bananas

Wash and drain the flaked rice. Bring the milk to a boil with the sugar, add the drained rice and cook until it is slightly thick and creamy. Add the cardamom and ghee and the bananas cut in thin slices. Cook, stirring, for a few minutes longer, then leave to get cold. The consistency should be that of a thin custard. Usually served as part of a vegetarian meal in the central and southern parts of India.

Ras Gulas
Cream Cheese Balls in Syrup (Bengal)   *Makes 10–12 balls*

8 cups milk	3 cups sugar
1 teaspoon tartaric acid	6 cups water
¾ cup hot water	10 cardamom pods, bruised
2 teaspoons fine semolina or plain flour	2 tablespoons rose water or few drops rose essence
pinch of bicarbonate of soda	
10–12 sugar cubes or a few crystals of rock sugar, optional	

In the huge kitchens of Hotel Ashoka in New Delhi one may see the most modern of Western appliances used in turning out Western style food, while in another part of the same room traditional methods of Indian cooking are employed to turn out Indian food that is as authentic as any cooked on a village fireplace in primitive clay pots or in the great earthen tandoor ovens. One large section is given over to a halvai (sweetmaker) who provides the hotel with authentic Indian sweetmeats.

In a large saucepan heat the milk to boiling point, stirring gently to prevent milk solids settling and scorching on base of pan. Dissolve tartaric acid in hot water. As milk starts to rise in the pan, add the tartaric acid solution, gradually, stirring until the milk curdles. Cover and set aside for 15 minutes, then strain through muslin and leave to drain for 20–30 minutes. (If milk does not curdle readily, add a little more tartaric acid, dissolved in water.) When whey has stopped dripping from the curds but *before the curds get too dry*, turn them into a bowl or onto a marble slab and knead vigorously for 5 minutes. Add semolina or plain flour and bicarbonate of soda and knead again until the cream cheese is smooth and the palm of the hand feels greasy. Divide into 10–12 equal portions and mould each one into a ball. If liked, mould around a sugar cube or a few grains of rock sugar.

Put sugar and water into a saucepan with the cardamom pods and bring to the boil, stirring to dissolve sugar. Boil hard for 5 minutes. Take 1 cup of this syrup and put into another pan. Add enough water to give a depth of about 5 cm (2 inches), and bring this to a fast boil. Put the cream cheese balls in, leaving enough room for them to swell as they almost double in size. Boil fast for 15–20 minutes, then lift out on slotted spoon and transfer to the warm syrup. Repeat with more of the cream cheese balls, until they are all done. Flavour the syrup they are soaking in with rose, and leave to soak overnight or at least 4 hours. Do not chill as they will lose their spongy texture.

Gajjar Halwa
Carrot Sweetmeat (Punjab)   *Makes about 20 pieces*

500 g (1 lb) carrots
60 g (2 oz) ghee
¼ teaspoon ground cardamom
1¼ cups sugar
½ cup hot water
1 cup cream

4 tablespoons dried milk
   powder or khoa (page xxi)
2 tablespoons blanched slivered
   almonds or pistachios
edible silver leaf (varak) to
   garnish, optional

Wash and peel carrots, then grate them finely. Heat ghee in a heavy saucepan and add the carrots. Cook uncovered over medium heat, stirring. Cover and turn heat very low, allowing carrots to cook in steam until soft and almost all the liquid has evaporated. Make a syrup by boiling the sugar and water. Add syrup to carrots and stir in the cream and milk powder or khoa, blending all the ingredients well. Cook, stirring constantly, until the mixture is thick enough to come away from sides of pan in one lump. Turn onto a greased dish, smooth top with buttered aluminium foil if necessary, and allow to cool. Decorate with almonds and pistachios and, if liked, with silver leaf. Cut into small diamond shapes or squares.

Gulab Jamun
Rose Flavoured Sweetmeats in Syrup
(Bengal)   *Makes about 18 (serves 6)*

8 tablespoons full cream milk
  powder
3 tablespoons self-raising flour
¼ teaspoon bicarbonate of soda
¼ teaspoon ground cardamom
1 tablespoon soft butter or ghee
approximately 3 tablespoons
  water
ghee or oil for deep frying

Syrup:
2 cups white sugar
4 cups water
5 cardamom pods, bruised
2 tablespoons rose water or
  few drops rose essence

*Gulab jamun look like small brown sausages but they taste heavenly –
sweet, rose-flavoured, rich with concentrated milk flavour – one of
the delicacies that has won for Bengal the reputation of making the
best Indian sweets.*

Sift milk powder, flour, bicarbonate of soda and ground cardamom
into a large bowl. Rub in butter or ghee, then add enough water to
give a firm but pliable dough which can be moulded into balls the
size of large marbles, or into small sausage shapes.

Heat ghee or oil flavoured with a little ghee and fry the shapes over
low heat until they slowly turn golden brown. Lift out on slotted
spoon and drain on absorbent paper.

Syrup: Before frying the gulab jamun, make the syrup by combining
sugar, water and cardamom pods and heating until sugar is
dissolved. Put the fried gulab jamun into the warm syrup and add
rose water when they have cooled somewhat. Leave for at least 4
hours, or overnight. The gulab jamun will swell and become soft and
spongy. Serve at room temperature or chilled.

Jalebi

Crisp Fried Batter Spirals (Gujarat)　　　　　　*Makes about 24*

Batter:
2 cups plain flour
½ cup ground rice or rice flour
7 g (¼ oz) fresh compressed
　yeast or scant teaspoon dried
　yeast
½ cup lukewarm water
¼ teaspoon saffron strands
2 tablespoons boiling water
1 tablespoon yoghurt
oil for deep frying

Syrup:
3 cups sugar
3 cups water
1 tablespoon light corn syrup
　or pinch cream of tartar
rose essence to flavour
1½ teaspoons liquid orange food
　colour

Sift the flour and ground rice into a large bowl. Sprinkle yeast on the lukewarm water in a small bowl, leave to soften for 5 minutes and stir to dissolve. Pound saffron strands in mortar and pestle, dissolve in boiling water.

Pour dissolved yeast and saffron water into a measuring jug. Add lukewarm water to make up to 2¼ cups. Stirring with a wooden spoon, add the liquid to the flour and beat well until batter is very smooth. Add yoghurt and beat again. Leave to rest for 1 hour. Batter will start to become frothy. Beat vigorously once more before starting to fry jalebis. (While batter is resting make the syrup and leave it to become just warm.)

Heat oil in a deep frying pan or a karahi and when hot pour in the batter using a small funnel, or in a cloth icing bag with a small opening. Make circles or figures of eight or a series of loops. Fry, turning once, until crisp and golden on both sides. Lift out on a slotted spoon, let the oil drain for a few seconds, then drop the hot jalebi into the syrup and soak it for a minute or two. Lift out of the syrup using another slotted spoon and put on a plate to drain.

Transfer jalebis to a clean plate and serve as soon as possible after making because their crispness diminishes after some time.

Syrup: Heat sugar and water over low heat, stirring until sugar dissolves. Raise heat and boil hard for 8 minutes. Syrup should be just thick enough to spin a thread. Remove from heat, allow to cool until lukewarm, flavour with rose essence and colour bright orange with food colouring.

Badam Kheer
Creamed Almonds (Uttar Pradesh)   *Serves: 4–5*

4 cups milk
1 cup cream
1 tablespoon ghee
1 cup almonds
6 tablespoons sugar
$\frac{1}{8}$ teaspoon saffron strands
2 tablespoons boiling water
$\frac{1}{4}$ teaspoon ground cardamom

Garnish:
flaked almonds, optional
edible silver leaf, optional

Put milk, cream and ghee into a saucepan and bring to the boil, stirring constantly. When it starts to boil turn the heat very low and let it simmer for 15 minutes, stirring occasionally. Meanwhile, bring the almonds to the boil in a small pan and boil for 2 or 3 minutes, then drain and plunge into cold water.

Slip off the skins and slice the almonds very thinly, using a vegetable peeler. If they are soft from being blanched this is easier to do. Alternatively, grind the almonds in an electric blender. Add almonds and sugar to the milk and cook, stirring. Pound saffron strands in a mortar and pestle, dissolve in the boiling water and add. Continue cooking until it is the consistency of custard. Remove from the heat, stir in cardamom, and pour into a dessert dish. Cover and chill before serving. If liked, garnish with a few extra flaked almonds and silver leaf.

lebele
Pancakes with Coconut Filling (Goa)   *Serves: 4*

2 eggs
½ cup milk
½ cup water
pinch salt
1 tablespoon melted butter
1 cup plain flour, sifted
butter or ghee for frying
raw cashews, roughly chopped,
    optional

Filling:
1 coconut, freshly grated
125 g (4 oz) jaggery or brown
    sugar

Some versions of the filling include a little lemon juice, a few sultanas, a pinch of crushed anise or a little grated fresh ginger, but I prefer the delicate coconut flavour on its own.

In a large bowl, beat the eggs lightly until combined but not frothy. Add milk, water, salt and melted butter and mix, then add all the flour and beat with a wooden spoon or rotary beater until smooth. Leave batter for 1 hour at least before cooking.

Grease a heavy pancake pan with butter or ghee, using only just enough to give a thin film. Pour in a small ladle of the batter and swirl the pan to coat the base thinly. Cook over medium heat until golden brown on the underside. Turn pancake over and cook other side for a few seconds. Turn onto a plate. Cook all the batter in this way, then fill each pancake with 2 tablespoons of the coconut filling and roll up. If liked, sprinkle with roughly chopped raw cashews.

Filling: Combine coconut with the jaggery which has been finely scraped with a knife or on a grater, or broken into pieces and pounded with mortar and pestle.

INDEX